An Unfinished Revolution

Kishalay Bhattacharjee is a senior journalist who has reported from India's conflict zones for over two decades. He has received several awards including the Ramnath Goenka Excellence in Journalism Award (2006–7) for his reportage of internally displaced people. His coverage of the abduction and rescue of two Italian tourists was nominated for the best current affairs programme by Association of International Broadcasting (AIB) Awards in 2013. He currently teaches in the School of Journalism and Communications at OP Jindal Global University in Sonipat, Haryana.

Also by Kishalay Bhattacharjee

Che in Paona Bazaar: Tales of Exile and Belonging from India's North-East

Blood on My Hands: Confessions of Staged Encounters

An Unfinished Revolution

A HOSTAGE CRISIS, ADIVASI RESISTANCE AND THE NAXAL MOVEMENT

Kishalay Bhattacharjee

PAN

First published in India 2017 by Macmillan
an imprint of Pan Macmillan Publishing India Private Limited
707, Kailash Building
26, K. G. Marg, New Delhi – 110 001
www.panmacmillan.co.in

Pan Macmillan, 20 New Wharf Road, London N1 9RR
Basingstoke and Oxford
Associated companies throughout the world
www.panmacmillan.com

ISBN 978-93-82616-37-5

1 3 5 7 9 8 6 4 2

Typeset by Manmohan Kumar
Printed and bound in India by
Replika Press Pvt. Ltd.

This book is for my mother and father who made me believe that books are the most precious possessions, and to my daughter Bambi who helps me find meaning in the mundane. This is also for the millions of Indians who challenge the odds in their daily revolutions.

Contents

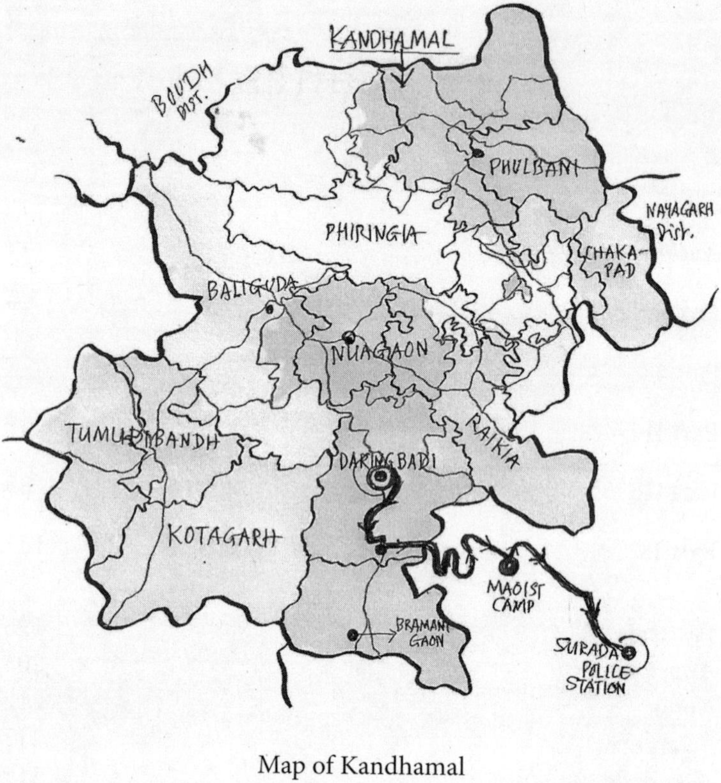

Map of Kandhamal

Author's Note

'At least we tried,' says Animesh Mitra, the cult literary Naxalite who came from small-town Jalpaiguri to Calcutta and got sucked into the 'revolution'. Released from jail after the Left Front came to power, Animesh is paraplegic due to severe torture and comes out of the prison to find his partner Madhobilata waiting for him. She is a struggling schoolteacher and lives in a one-room shanty with their six-year-old son Arko.

– Samaresh Majumder, *Uttoradhikar, Kalbela*[1] and *Kalpurush* (a searing account of Naxal Bengal of the 1970s)

When I was growing up in the 1970s and '80s, Bengali literature, to which I was more exposed than perhaps that of any other language, had two fundamental themes – Partition and the Naxal uprising. The novels and accounts I read then left an indelible impression on my young mind about the need for a revolution and 'class struggle' – that had begun as it were in Naxalbari where peasant guerilla movements were organized as a means of capturing power. Led by the revolutionary communists, the idea of the working class claiming power and changing the world appeared immensely seductive to the peasants. They were then referred to as Naxals and as a group, believing in the 'annihilation of class enemies' and Chairman Mao's ideology, they were later rechristened as Maoists.

I have spent most of my working life so far studying the lives of people in what we casually refer to as 'conflict zones'. The Adivasis living along what the government calls the 'Maoist corridor' and the eight states referred to as India's North East are among them. I gathered that the people in the Maoist corridor are marginalized in every way, and have only themselves and their spoken words to indicate who they are. Ethnographers and anthropologists will have different perspectives and methodologies when trying to interpret these people. As a journalist and chronicler, I approached them through a completely different route.

For a broadcast journalist, writing a book is like editing a film with an abundance of visual footage from where one must choose the sequences and the points of view to tell the story. I was sure whose story I would be telling – Claudio's of course – but I also had to ponder deeply to understand the questions, the whys and wherefores surrounding the Adivasis which led to Claudio's crisis.

In 2011, I was appointed Chair, Internal Security, and Senior Fellow at the Institute for Defence Studies and Analyses in New Delhi. I wanted to pursue field-based research to see what the state response has been towards long-running insurgencies in India, the CPI (Maoist) being one of them. My view was that in the absence of a national policy to address such insurrections, the state has been engaged in a protracted ad hoc mechanism of dealing with the resistance without really addressing the problem. To study this, I visited Koraput and Malkangiri in Odisha. I also wanted to explore the dynamics the Adivasis have with the extreme left-wing Maoists. I was certain that viewing Adivasis as Maoists or Maoist sympathizers is a stereotype we have perpetuated and that Maoists have only found Adivasis a convenient and vulnerable group to help sustain the party.

When I reached Malkangiri, I was confronted by monuments of Maoist control – brick-red three-storeyed tombs of 'Maoist martyrs'. Several such monuments dot the landscape. Maoist signposts and welcome plaques were common sights. This is what the then Indian prime minister, Dr Manmohan Singh, may have meant in his address at a chief ministers' meet on Naxalism in 2006 when he said, 'They are trying to establish "liberation zones" in core areas where they are dispensing or claiming to be dispensing basic state functions of administration, policing and justice. It is a cause for great concern that civil administration and police are periodically absent in some of these areas.'

On the ground, the Maoists are seen as opportunists. They are very organized. For example, they raise issues of development but at the same time they vehemently oppose any developmental activity. Their organizational strength has been tested at various levels. A beleaguered police force has no confidence to take them on. The police believe that areas such as Koraput and Malkangiri will continue to be safe havens and the Maoists will not launch major offensives as long as they are allowed to operate in an administrative vacuum. The government seems okay with that.

In 2012, I had the extraordinary opportunity of joining an excursion into an Adivasi settlement in Odisha to follow the story of two Italian men abducted by the Maoists operating in the area. In that impossible trek through the jungles of Kandhamal, I found the anchor to the stories I had been researching and trying to tell.

The idea of the book came a year later when I was touring with my first book *Che in Paona Bazaar*, in which I tried to weave a series of real-life stories from a conflict zone to connect some dots that defy all stereotypes. I was thinking of the dots in the Maoist–Adivasi resistance, a story that is as old as I am today and a story with which I have literally grown up.

In the course of my research at the Nehru Memorial Museum and Library in New Delhi, I was going through reams and reams of pages on the Maoist/Naxal 'uprising' and tribal resistance, but couldn't identify a definitive study that explored the protracted Maoist movement woven with the Adivasi struggle and its reality. I imagined that if I pegged the hostage crisis I was a part of in the larger Maoist movement, it could perhaps provide an on-the-ground understanding of 'tribal militancy' and the Maoist 'revolution' that is still 'unfinished'.

In that sense, this book is part reportage, part personalized ethnography and part memoir. I didn't choose Kandhamal, it happened to me. I chose Koraput and Malkangiri because of their strategic importance given how they blur the Odisha, Jharkhand, Andhra and Chhattisgarh borders and this is where the Maoists find their roots. I wanted to see these places as an integral part of larger political and historical institutions but from the ground, up close and intimate.

In this book, I have tried to describe the kinds of experiences we have had in our coverage of the hostage crisis not only from my point of view, but through the many parties involved in it: the hostages, the inhabitants and the Maoists themselves. I believe the conversations and arguments provide a fresh window to the tribal world, the conflict within and a war that has been studied in isolation for years.

Every story or history has multiple realities: what really happened and the various perceptions of what happened. It has facts and figures – sometimes incorrect – and then images and words wherein the facts and figures find their place.

Unfortunately, much of what is known today is through mass media that records real-time stories and shapes perceptions. It is like a self-generating cell that spreads through the body polity. As a journalist reporting conflict, I felt I had the power to tell the story the way I wanted to and thus create the image I wanted to project. This is dangerous because the limits of depiction and the language of mass media deny the unimaginable and unspeakable. It may repudiate the thread of history in picking and choosing the story and the location according to its own liking. For instance, a masked Maoist carrying a gun would invariably be an Adivasi man or woman – that is both correct as well as incorrect. The recognizable image is indeed erroneous, but to point out the error would require an understanding of how this image was created and how it has sustained itself.

It would be useful to refer to the February 1856 issue of *The Illustrated London News* which featured sketches of the 'Suppression of Santhal Insurrection' of 1855–56 by Captain Walter Stanhope Sherwill,[2] a revenue surveyor of the British government in India, that created the perception of Santhals as criminals. The visual discourse on counterinsurgency has often been mediated by coercive agents of the state and later, after the suppression of the insurgency, passed on by the same agents to more popular forces such as mass media.

Halfway through the book, I returned to my fieldwork in the Koraput–Malkangiri area of Odisha, travelling through India's 'liberated zones'. I had started my work imagining that the Naxal movement was only a story of splits and mergers, with violence as its guiding principle, but in that journey I was absorbed by the utter deprivation of a people whose own history of resistance was conveniently appropriated by the Naxals. These people had lost the ability to speak for themselves and, if they did, it was seen as dissent that needed to be crushed by both sides wielding guns.

Past and present are juxtaposed in this narrative of a hostage crisis, the fifty-year-old Maoist/Naxal movement and the tribal resistance which spans over 200 years and one that is a continuing story. It is not a book of history or ethnography, but a preview of an India that is perceived as very remote and primitive.

When I decided to revisit Naxalbari, West Bengal, in 2014 to meet Shanti Munda – the only surviving 'comrade' of the 'uprising' – my then fourteen-year-old daughter asked me about the significance of the place. I told her and she was curious how such an important milestone finds no mention in her history book. This is more than an oversight, because the Adivasi story is only referred to when a bomb explodes or an ambush kills and security persons are sent in to dominate the conflict zone.

The world has changed out of measure and the revolutionary literature I was steeped in has since moved in new directions. However, the stereotypical representations of the Adivasis have only deepened. The exploitation has become institutionalized and the Maoists have sustained their business of violence because of this. There is no change in the horizon but it may be useful to put these facts into perspective to understand why the heartland of India's geography is the source of the longest conflict between the people and the state.

Prologue

He does not seem to accept defeat easily and wants to play another game but that too ends in the same manner. In a rather comical and puerile way, he then tries to change the pieces on the board, claiming strange rules.

There is little conversation between the two chess players now. One's face is taut, striving to appear in control, and the other victorious but indifferent. The chessboard is perched on a dead tree trunk lying on the ground. Both players straddle the trunk, with cotton towels over their faces to keep away the harsh sun and the buzzing flies. Around them people carry on with their chores, paying no attention to the two men in their forties, battling it out with their respective armies.

Someone comes up and wants to share something with him and he finds another excuse to restart the game, saying he has been distracted. He catches my friend making a move while he is talking and says that it is against the rules. He recasts his strategies and castling moves. The gun by his side is of little use in trying to protect his kingdom on the chessboard. In three moves my friend throws his horseman out and advances the army towards the palace gates. The gunman's elephants are not good enough to defend the gates and give way to an unstoppable brigade. This is the third successive defeat he is on the verge of suffering and each one makes him more irritable. But he will not go down fighting. He gets up before the game is over and announces that it is time for him to get some work done, indicating that if he continues he would have surely defeated my friend.

•

It is surreal. In the middle of a jungle in Kandhamal in Odisha, where it is unbelievably hot and humid, two men – an abductor and a captive – are engrossed in a game of chess. The hostage is winning repeatedly and the captor is frustrated with defeat after defeat. The captive's life hangs on the whims of the captor whose existential crisis now is about losing chess matches to a man he holds prisoner. He feeds the hostage fruits and cashew nuts and bread and butter with mashed potatoes, bartering their lives for his demands. And he hates to lose.

The hostage belongs to a different world, thousands of kilometres away, and the captor is the commander of an armed underground left-wing extremist party that has been fighting the Indian security forces for years. Held at gunpoint with no certainty about his life, the hostage challenges the captor to this series of games and hands out a humiliating defeat.

While they are at play, hundreds of people are searching for them. Television networks are playing up the news every day – of the 'abduction drama' and 'hostage crisis'. Negotiators are having endless sessions with the government authorities. Security forces are planning their next move. But here, under the scorching sun in a burning forest, where there is danger of an attack every moment, the chess players play on, oblivious to their surroundings.

PART I

23 March 2012

A bustling market where townspeople meet to discuss life and other mundane things over tiny cups of tea, flat rice with gram and vadas with sambar. A tar road leads from the intersection towards the forest guest house, one of the few landmarks of the town. The place has hardly any accommodation to offer to the more than forty journalists and photographers camping in the township. In one of the alleys is a house where we have been staying for the past one week. Kailash Dandapat runs an NGO, Jagruti, from this house. Dandapat is a middle-aged man who is very hospitable and helpful. He avoids political discussions but is always enthusiastic about sharing any other information.

He had put us up in a very hot room with two single beds and a narrow strip for a bathroom. The house is a one-storey concrete structure with a large dormitory and two other rooms. The backyard has a well, a garden of jackfruit and mango trees, and a vegetable patch. Across the fence are fields where the paddy is growing. Beyond the fields the hills start rising.

For days, we had made the small room he had given us our home. Three people could be under mosquito nets on the two beds, while the one sleeping on the floor had to cover his face with a sheet to escape mosquito bites. The temperature goes up to 48 degrees and there are regular power cuts for long hours. This is the 'suite' in the house; the other hall is like a dormitory accommodating scores of other journalists who had arrived after the news of the abduction. None of them have ever heard of this place nor did they have any idea what to do once they got here. So they just waited for news of the release. In these areas, one doesn't venture out much without the permission of the Maoists themselves.

Mornings are early because nights are insufferable and the only cool air is an hour before sunrise. It is during this early morning hour that the town market temporarily livens up with gossip from the district headquarters on local development and contractor funds. The night bus from Bhubaneswar also arrives during this time. Rows of food stalls serve hot sambar, vada, dosa and various other snacks including kheer. The food is served in bowls and dishes made of *siyali patta*, leaves, the only cash trade the tribal villagers engage in. They make leaf bowls and dishes and bring them to the market every day to earn a little money.

A few hundred feet from the market is the police station where Claudio and Paulo had registered their arrival before they disappeared. They were apparently warned of Maoist activity in the region. But Maoist activity is not some flag march of a uniformed army that carries on all the time so they ignored the cautionary message and proceeded. There is nothing, absolutely nothing to indicate that there is danger ahead.

In Glass Garden, the only restaurant in the town, journalists gather for lunch and early dinner. The way the food is served is interesting: bowls of paneer, chicken, vegetables, fritters and dal come in a huge tray which is placed in the middle of the table. The man at the counter looks like his father in the photograph on the wall behind him, garlanded with withered flowers. They do brisk business here. The Italian abduction is not a matter of interest, neither is Maoism. But two kilometres away the soundscape changes if you were to venture out. There are no signposts, no landmines or even police patrol but the dissonance with the rest of the world is what strikes one at first.

Daringbari is infamous for poor cell phone connectivity. The network comes once a week and the blame is laid on the state machinery that prefers it to be a blind zone so that Naxal communication is affected. And recently, cables were snapped while road construction work was going on and therefore it has become a zone of no communication. Within the town limits, the insiders and outsiders engage in speculations about the abduction and release of two men about whom people know very little. A lot of the talk is about why they were in such a nondescript part of the country. Some say they were sent by Indian intelligence agencies to spy on Maoist hideouts. Others say foreigners come to sexually exploit tribal women. While one man who claims deep insights into the developments orders another glass of tea and nods his head twice to dismiss all opinions; he pronounces, in a tone of finality, that the Maoists staged this abduction with the help of their Italian comrades to escape from the heat of police operations and get some of the comrades freed.

Daringbari is also known for snow during winter, a rather curious climatic phenomenon given Odisha's terrain. It is a township that is somehow lost in itself, a tea break for long-distance travels across the state. Its anonymity helps the Maoists to operate with little or no administrative disruption. This is probably the first time the town has been witness to so much activity, with hordes of media crew all over the place.

About fifteen TV outside broadcast vans of various local and national networks have been hounding us for almost a week, assuming that we have news from the jungle. Each time we step out, we are tracked. Yes, we are hopeful of news reaching us first, but not a word has come to us in almost a week now.

The morning holds a very good chance, so we quietly prepare ourselves, mostly keeping indoors so as to not give away our excitement.

By noon I ask one of the team members to fetch a few essentials we may need. Our preparations involve a few oranges, bottles of water and some dry fruits. These are not the usual precautionary steps that anybody should follow in such circumstances, but in the absence of any mandatory guidelines we take things casually, possibly putting ourselves at grave risk. The indication we had received was that the hideout was quite close by and it would take all of four hours to return with the news.

Around 3 p.m., the missive arrives and we discreetly step out of that hot, insufferable room and drive out in the red jeep as if to grab some lunch in Glass Garden. Instead of getting off we veer into an alley and through the back lanes of a row of houses to arrive at the road adjacent to the police station. It would take us to our destination. As the vehicle moves up an incline we are spotted by a motorcycle-borne man who slows down a few seconds but then speeds in the direction he was headed. We ignore the warning sign.

Though it is March, it is a scorching summer's 4 p.m. The villages look half deserted and hungry. The homes are shanty and it is an unlikely hour for city vehicles to travel on this road. The narrow stretch across the ghat meanders through pine trees and arrives at ginger fields. The last shop on this route is a dhaba that agrees to serve us some scrambled eggs and rice-based hard balls. There are no other customers. The charcoal fire heating our tea is now an ember; perhaps it's time for them to shut down.

Before we can even finish our meagre lunch, a convoy of the TV outside broadcast vans accompanied by many other vehicles arrive with almost a vengeance. The man on the motorcycle must have carried the news to the eager crowd of people on the prowl. We have been caught and now we can no longer proceed. We pretend to shoot the dhaba, speaking to the owners and locals around, going about our business as it were. We say we want to do a story on turmeric and ginger. It is not convincing at all and we give in, admitting that yes, we have information but clearly that is going to be of no use since we are now exposed and therefore we are aborting the operation. Our planning was flawed but this is the best we could have done under the circumstances.

After attempting to impress upon the several crews of journalists that it is ridiculous to follow a Maoist trail with an entourage of four-dozen men, we pretend to give up on the opportunity and start driving back to the base, though not before promising that if we manage to get any information we would share some of it. At an intersection, we take a U-turn and this time nobody chases us. This is our final chance and we find ourselves back on the trail we were meant to take towards the hideout. We are already late and that is not good.

We reach a culvert and wonder if this is where the red jeep is supposed to halt, open its bonnet and wait for further signs – they had specified that it should be the red jeep only. There are two culverts on the way and there is no way to determine where to halt. A private contractor is supervising road construction in an area where nobody ventures without prior approval of the people in control. Instructions here are given in bits and pieces but followed very carefully.

After a long wait we spot a man twirling his cap around his finger and sauntering towards the vehicle. But he walks past without giving us any signals. We get down, restlessly pacing around a half-constructed community centre and some houses with curious onlookers, though it is not advisable to be out in public in this way. Information about outsiders in these parts travels very fast.

A little later, almost camouflaged against the sparse forest, two tribal men in torn clothes discreetly signal us to follow them. One of them is in a lungi and a holey vest, the other in dirty oversized trousers and a torn red T-shirt, his face half covered with a red chequered cotton towel. One is tall and the other short; one won't smile, while the other can't stop grinning.

A few paces along the track and the road is no longer visible behind us. Ahead, the forest appears broken. The men stop and hand over a thin stick no longer than six centimetres. Without uttering a word, they indicate that the stick be broken in the middle. It is a hollow twig that snaps easily. We look at them, puzzled, holding the broken stick. One of them indicates where to look: inside one end of the stick is a piece of rolled paper tied with a thread. The paper is a letter welcoming us to the jungles with a brief warning that the number of people should not exceed six and no one should have followed or seen us. We were six; my colleagues Sampad Mahapatra and Biswajit Das and then Sandeep Sahu, Subhrakanta Nayak and Dayanidhi Dash. On our way up here, we were indeed spotted but we let that pass. As soon as the note is read, the taller of the two guides takes the paper back and chews it up, leaving no evidence.

We are now walking on uneven, trackless terrain, with burned and slashed vegetation. It feels as though we've entered the heart of the forest almost immediately. The heat is intense. Both the guides move ahead as the flat land suddenly meets a steep slope that one can cross only by running down. Each of us has been given a stick to help us walk on the rough terrain. At the base of the slope is a grove of prickly plants which we negotiate to emerge in a clearing with a water body. There are no human or animal or bird sounds. It is still and dull. With the sun about to set, the walk is now uphill.

Drinking water is already running out. The plan was to return in four hours but now it seems a remote possibility. The guides will not speak and so there is no way of knowing how long this will take. After two hours of traversing that uneven surface, everybody is weary and thirsty. I hold back a few oranges I had carried in my backpack. One crew member has high blood pressure and his legs are giving up, the other has an excruciating backache. I feel it is a suicide mission to go on further.

The light drops with one stroke and the unprepared crew can now barely walk. With the tight-lipped guides unwilling to give us a breather, the camera lights come to the rescue showing us the path ahead. There is no hint of a breeze, no light source in the distance, and the only sounds are the crackle of dead leaves beneath our feet and our heavy breathing. Tired feet trip on the incline and people fall over each other, but there is no time to sit and rest. One must walk. This is a cattle track where the animals walk on a horizontal line on the slope. It appears that we are nearing the edge of the forest but at every turn we take there is more darkness ahead. The heat seems to be increasing and the body surrendering to the sapping walk. If there was an option we would have abandoned this trek and returned. Now it is too late.

Every minute is stretched in time and every unwilling step seems to extend the route further.

At last, the forest clears out. Ahead, enveloped in pitch darkness, is probably a paddy field. The land is now flat and the earth is softer. Tired bodies throw themselves on the damp grass experiencing an almost hallucinatory effect. Are we really where we are? Where are we? Did we walk all evening or was that just a delirious dream? There is not a drop of water to drink; the oranges had to be given away to others. But there is little respite. The guides won't let us rest and recover, saying there is a village nearby and any sound at this hour of the night will wake them up. Alarmed villagers could mean news travelling out. The tungsten camera lights had to be put out lest we are identified. So we are led through pitch dark marshy land and it is as bad as walking blindfolded.

We walk through streams and trees and fields rising up and coming down like a bumpy road leading to the dark sky. An unknown force pushes the walkers ahead and there is no turning back; one must move on. The guides are now using a slim torch with blue illumination, the kind used in the villages. It is the last lap of the journey, or so one is told.

In batches of two, people are being taken through a grove. Sandeep, a fellow journalist, is familiar with this terrain, but being unwell, is finding it difficult to carry on. However, there is no option but to move forward. Sandy's cell phone plays a few Kishore Kumar songs to overcome the eeriness. The battery dies out and it is the forest night sounds again. Glowworms keep us company. We are no longer trying to keep up any enthusiasm; we are not even looking at each other, leave alone talking. We know this has been a huge mistake.

Finally, there's a village where everyone rushes for the well. Buckets full of water are poured on the head and hands to cool ourselves down and everybody takes turns to quench the last few hours of thirst. The sensation of water on skin and the knowledge that we are amongst people is reassuring. We are seated on the verandah of a school and there is hardly any conversation. The legs are numb and the bodies stretch themselves to regain some equilibrium. The village is asleep and one of the guides is now replaced. The shorter of the two stays on and a brash young boy joins in. He does not appear friendly and is used to giving instructions. He probably has a gun on him.

We are now huddled into one mud-baked room with some farming implements and hanging clothes and a cooking corner with the remnants of dinner. Its owner, a village schoolmaster, we are informed, has gone on leave. It is dark and we are now allowed to switch on the camera light.

A dinner of dal with potatoes and rice has been served and strict instructions have been left by the new guide to sleep early. Before daybreak the journey must resume. After dinner, the plates are taken away and some water provided to wash our hands in the backyard.

With just a couple of hours left for daybreak, fidgety bodies try to get some rest though they are angry at the breach of promise; the four-hour journey has already become eight and there is no clarity on when and where this would end. The crew can hardly talk but sleep does not come easily with extreme exhaustion. Cigarette smoke should not carry to villagers because apparently the residents do not know of the presence of strangers. The half night is spent tossing about, filled with uncertainty.

24 March 2012

Before daybreak, the village is already waking up as the guides force the crew to start moving. In the haze of the dawn, the village looks like a smoky watercolour about to burst into activity. Most of the houses are barely holding their walls together. A woman is pounding rice on her verandah and another two are drawing water from the well. They pretend not to notice me. We must not be seen by anyone, but surely, they know who we are and why we are here.

A herd of cows leave early for grazing, moving in the direction from where we arrived last evening. In the morning light, the area is no longer as frightening as it had seemed when we were forced to walk in the dark. The trees now appear in rows and and the undulating terrain with the paddy fields and streams is rather pretty. Night has its own invincibility and the mere inability to see through the darkness makes it terrifying. The team takes the road that travels below the village. It is unlikely that the villagers did not sense our arrival and departure. The police surely will have informers amongst them as well, hence the cautious movements to escape notice.

It is downhill now. The terrain is slightly different and daylight brings some hope. The team stops at a large stream to wash and defecate and freshen themselves up before another unending walk. There is a clearing with stone benches for traveller to rest. It is a serene morning and the sun rises from a range of hills, a tall tree silhouetted against it.

Unlike yesterday's journey, this one is along a track used by villagers but precarious for outsiders not used to such terrain – narrow ridges between massive boulders hanging halfway into nothing. The sticks are ornamental swords to motivate the team members but of no use on the slippery ground. With nothing to eat or drink and a steep rocky mountain to cross and half the crew feeling sick, the journey is getting increasingly worrying. The guides are not happy with the slow progress of the crew but they say nothing. We pass by haystacks, ramshackle huts and burned grass. An odd villager is seen walking by but carefully bypasses our route perhaps to avoid any conversation with the guides. Nobody likes to talk to guns.

After hours of tumbling up and down there is some flat land and a dirty stream from where the plastic bottles are refilled. I have given up hoping for anything at all – water, food, a story or even our safety. These areas are mined and it feels as though we are being constantly monitored by invisible eyes to ensure we are not government agents. The guides still haven't revealed how far we are going and how long it will take. How long can we hold on? It is an utterly frustrating, insane situation to be in. Caught in a time warp, these self-styled guerillas live with their own outdated notions of changing the world. They have no idea what they want or where they are headed. We all rant in our heads but we know we have brought this upon ourselves.

The three sick team members are given a thatched shelter to catch some sleep while the rest carry on. A knee-deep stream has to be crossed. But the flow of water is strong. At one point while I am halfway across the water trying to balance on the wet rocks, the guides disappear with a warning that the police may be ahead. They have spotted the marks of canvas shoes on the dusty village road. There is a possibility that we have been followed. Villagers would have seen us driving and the convoy of journalists who came after us could have given the police some leads. It is also possible that some of them may have gone back and reported our movement to the police. Either way we could be in real trouble.

We are told to keep walking and if confronted by the security forces we would have to make up a story. It is unlikely they would believe our story. One look at us and they would know we don't have a clue where we are. Quite often security forces target journalists in conflict zones alleging that we help the cause of the militants. Many have been intimidated and even killed. If we are caught here they could easily shoot us, saying it was an encounter.

With no sign of the guides, we decide to catch some rest against the rocks by the stream. The weariness, hunger, heat and thirst are almost too much. There is no evidence of police anywhere. The nearby village is not surprised at the presence of strangers or maybe they are trained to not react to new faces. I go around the village looking for the guides and filling some more water from the bore well pump. Villagers notice me but they look the other way. I walk like a zombie and now nothing matters as long as I can get some sleep. Every fibre of the body is resisting any further walks. The mind is lifeless. I want to throw myself in the dirty stream and just lie there. Only flowing water can cure me now.

One of the guides emerge from nowhere and lead us a few paces across the stream into a clearing.

At last two young men in lungis carrying guns can be spotted, indicating the destination must be close. They have charpoys and they serve a welcome drink of glucose water along with biscuits. There is no hurry in their movements but this is surely not the place where we were supposed to have reached the previous evening. The men appear pleasant but there is little communication so the uncertainty continues. They keep smiling with an air of authority that can only come from the guns hanging by their side.

My body slumps over the charpoy in weary numbness. But, uncomfortable amidst these people, I sit up though I can't help reclining intermittently. The men talk amongst themselves, move towards the forest and speak on the radio; this exercise continues for some time till they all start looking stupid to me. I am just watching them inertly. I want to throttle them, take their guns and tell them it is not a joke, but I can barely move.

I try speaking to them but we don't understand each other. We try to impress upon them the urgency of meeting their commander or whoever is their head as well as bringing up the rest of the team who were left behind. Some food would help, we tell them. But it is hard to determine whether the men have understood us. They just smile stubbornly. After several minutes of anxious radio messages, the three of us are led up a hill track that winds through ancient boulders and dead leaves. Two other men with guns and faces covered are sitting on guard and there is nothing else to disturb the hot and humid air.

Patience has already run out but that is of little help in trying to convey the urgency. I'm not even sure whether we have reached our destination. I kick the leaves, as I have been doing through most of our torturous journey, and look around. It feels like we've been taken captive and are searching for ways to escape, with the captor sadistically enjoying our predicament. There is absolutely no doubt in my head now that this is a bunch of dangerous, sadistic and masochistic people who have created a make-believe kingdom exploiting the timid villagers.

The two men who had received us with biscuits and sugar water arrive with big pots on their heads – food has finally come. Some barely edible rice, dal and some vegetables are served. With deathly hunger, however, this makes for a sumptuous lunch. Water comes in camouflage flasks and nobody wastes a drop of water here. Food and water are very scarce in the arid jungle.

After lunch, I lean against a huge boulder to try to get some rest. It is afternoon and we have spent almost twenty-four hours in the custody of these men without a clue of the people we are meant to meet. Just then, I spot a middle-aged man in army fatigues walking down. He has a digital camera, a gun, a radio set with a long antenna and even a laptop. Two uniformed women are accompanying him, black meshes covering their faces. He speaks in hushed tones, a scarf concealing much of his face. He is hardly convincing, or even intimidating, but has an air of being in charge of the make-believe kingdom.

After ensuring that his face would not be photographed he unmasks himself and sits down for discussions. Though our initial grievance of why a four-hour trek became a sixteen-hour painful walk is ignored, his warm, friendly manner almost makes up for the terrifying time we've experienced. He is reminded about the team members we've left behind and he tells us that they are being brought here. His authority is stamped everywhere. I am disappointed with myself for not confronting him strongly about why we are being tortured in this manner, but I have reached my exhaustion threshold and I can't afford an argument now. Besides, it is fruitless.

It is almost evening in the hot and humid forest, and it is obvious we are not returning in a hurry.

Swarms of flies hit the face constantly, making it difficult to have a simple conversation. Now I understand the mystery of the black mesh covering the faces of the female cadres; it is a clever way of warding off the flies.

Staged between huge rocks with a jungle as the backdrop, the commander is ready to take questions. A surreal conversation begins between two strangers about two other strangers. The location, unknown and fraught with risk; suddenly there are mountain echoes of bullet shots. Was the crew being trailed or has the crew been planted by government forces to identify his camp? The commander gets into action, making radio calls, finding out where the sound came from. After anxious minutes of investigation, he finds out that it was the sound of tin sheets blown by a strong dust wind that echoed in the mountains. Assured by his comrades and happy in the knowledge that his plan – of making us walk through a maze of mountains to get here – has worked, he settles down again.

Kishalay Bhattacharjee (KB): Why did you abduct the Italians? Your fight is against the state which you claim represses the people here, so why Italians?

Commander (C): [in a muffled voice because of the chequered scarf covering his face to hide it from the camera] Some people, foreign and national tourists, and the government, have been trying to project the tribals as a commodity, as a subject of tourism. They are opening liquor shops in tribal areas, taking photographs. They treat the tribals like monkeys in a zoo.

For a while now the issue of intrusive tourism in tribal India has been making headlines: allegations that tourists, both foreign and Indian, even security forces, lure poor men and women with money or food and make them do their bidding.

Paolo Bosusco and Claudio Colangelo are accused of taking objectionable pictures of tribal women. The two Italians were camping near Kerubadi to study tribal life. The pictures seized, however, are nothing objectionable. The commander shows the photos on the display of the seized camera. There are some portraits of tribal men and women, a landscape, villagers doing their daily work but nothing that I can call 'objectionable' or voyeuristic. But the Maoist stand is that if you are not taking pictures of non-tribals moving around then why this enduring interest in tribals alone?

The Italians came here with a driver and local guide to take photos and notes on the tribal way of life. The driver and guide have already been released. The Maoist commander insists that the Italians' activities were suspicious. Not just suspicion, this is also political compulsion. Tribals are their strongest support bases and to retain that hold Maoists actively support their causes or generate some to justify their existence. Be it the displacement of tribals by mines and minerals' giants, their anger over lack of development or the current issue about their alleged exploitation by tourists, the Maoists act like their self-styled guardians.

The flies' attack on the face is irritating and I'm constantly fanning myself with a scarf to conduct this interview. The commander seems used to this way of life – of heat and flies and danger.

KB: They are exploiting by clicking pictures, you say, but don't you think you are also exploiting tribals and their underdevelopment by recruiting them, taking them away from their right to get educated or other rights?

C: Any movement has to be organized around economic issues. For a long time, the state has been suppressing the tribals and the poor people. They have a vision that this movement can free them from exploitation. So they come. So, it is economic issues and state repression that pushes them to us. If not for state repression, I couldn't have run this operation. It is an irony that our existence is because of a brutal state. Who would I have been able to recruit in these jungles? If the government just played its part by sincerely granting equal rights and refrained from rape and torture, this movement would die a natural death. It's quite simple, really.

The people don't know anything about Maoism. Look at her. She is Laxmi – one of my bodyguards. She's a very good fighter and she attends church every week. I don't stop them or give them lectures on communism.

KB: So if they don't follow or believe in your ideology, aren't you fooling them to believe in something else, maybe retributive violence?

C: Look at her, she is one of the members of my strike force, do you know why she is here? Rebecca is a local Kondh Christian tribal girl, one of my bodyguards. She is the one who led the team that arrested Claudio and Paolo.

Rebecca's face is covered with a black mesh not necessarily to conceal her identity but, as I said, as a defence against the swarms of insects buzzing around the face. It is a malaria-infested tropical jungle; everything here is scarce from water to food to healthcare. To avoid identification, Rebecca and her team must be constantly on the move through inhospitable terrain.

Slinging an automatic rifle, she carries a big pot of water or perhaps food as she walks down a treacherous path strewn with dead leaves. These are makeshift camps where cadres spend the night, barely catching some sleep, but that is a way of life. Camouflaged by unusually huge boulders and occupied also by families of monkeys, the hideout is ringed by villages that are loyal to the armed group. Women play the traditional role of cooking, cleaning and nursing along with the responsibilities of warfare.

Rebecca's sister had joined the organization and was arrested; she was allegedly gang-raped in police custody in the presence of her father who was forced to watch it. Then her brother was picked up by the security forces and died mysteriously, again in police custody. She says there was only one road left for her and that was to join the Maoists and seek revenge. Her story finds resonance in most women taking up arms in the Maoist ranks; state repression, they say, is what drives them to kill.

The Maoist document asserts: 'The history of oppressed women is the real history of the dearest daughters of our beloved country which is an inseparable, vital component of the history of oppressed people. And no success in the revolutionary war or the final victory of the revolution is imaginable or possible without women.' The document lists the numbers of rapes and tortures of women and says 'liberation from patriarchy' is the main reason for them joining the organization.

The ideological attraction of women from Indian universities towards this 'movement' in 1960–70 has given way to more real and desperate situations that prevail in the countryside: escape from poverty and fear of rape and atrocities by security forces. There are other factors as well, for example, local issues of displacement that affect the women who are predominantly the breadwinners of the family; they become vulnerable as they step out in search of work. Violence against women in India has been rising at an alarming rate and women like Rebecca are the most obvious victims.

In 2005 the introduction of Salwa Judum, an irregular force of local tribal population set up by some state governments to counter the Maoist militants, changed the course of anti-Maoist operations. Setting the tribals' against their own proved counterproductive. The Salwa Judum volunteers went on a rampage, looting villages and raping women. In desperation, women turned to the Maoists and many joined them. Since tribal society is women dominated, it is not unnatural for women to be part of what is largely a tribal-dominated guerrilla force. And here every girl has a story to tell, invariably of harassment.

KB: But what about harassment stories within your own units? You have been forcibly recruiting people as well. Isn't that harassment? Many women cadres, I am told, have reported that their male colleagues have abused them and leaders have used them?

C: The party has taken measures to address it but there are serious issues in that policy which I have openly challenged and I am not someone they like any longer. For example, they had a diktat that all women must shave their pubic hair. That is bizzare! Are they serious about the movement or have they lost it? And it is also said that all should bathe without clothes. What is the relation between revolution and such stupid theories, I cannot understand.

Maoists recruit women in their platoons for stability in armed formation and to keep a vigil on the male cadres who may harass villagers, which would go against their objective. Many women also have relatives in different formations. Yes, we do request every household in tribal areas to give one child. Many prefer to give the daughter, sending the son to a nearby town or city to earn a livelihood. In effect, almost half the fighting force now has women and most of the men and women cohabit either as married or unmarried couples. But there is a complete ban on having children and both men and women go through compulsory sterilisation. That does not mean there is no abuse.

This story has resonance. I recall meeting Rampati Ganjhu who was a sub-area commander of the Gaya CPI (Maoist) unit in Bihar and had spent fifteen years with the Maoists. Rampati had said, 'We had women from sixteen to forty years of age and almost all of those I knew had experienced some form of sexual abuse or exploitation. When they approached the police very few received any help. These women joined us to seek revenge but things are very different now. The only direction given by Maoist leaders now is to collect money through extortion that they themselves keep. More and more cadres are disillusioned and women in particular are being abused by the male leaders.'

Rashmi Mahli who I met once was lucky to escape and has since been covered under the government's rehabilitation offer. An active member of the Kundan Pahan group (Maoist) in the state of Jharkhand for sixteen years, Rashmi now runs a tea shop in the town of Ranchi that the government helped her set up. But like many of her colleagues who left the jungle she faces discrimination. Her story of taking up the gun because of poverty is a familiar one among the tribals there.

'We were seven siblings – five sisters, two brothers. We lived on meagre land produce and on many days, we would eat just one meal. Ours was a remote village in Bundu. From drinking water to proper roads – we had nothing. The Maoists would visit our village to recruit cadres. They had promised steady income for my family. There was no other way but to join them. I trained in small arms but I was not happy. I married a fellow Naxalite and we had a child. That changed my life. I couldn't live like that with my child. We were always in hiding and on the run. I wanted to surrender and live peacefully.'

Women generally play a tactical role in operations. They are placed at the front to distract security forces. Some of the major Maoist attacks had women leading from the front. In Chhattisgarh, the attack on a convoy of political leaders in 2013 also had women at the front; it was one of the biggest ambushes by the Maoists in recent times in the country.

KB: But why do you recruit only tribals? Like the ryots historically exploited the tribals, you too find them easy prey, don't you?

C: I am not using them. We empower them to stand up for their rights. As far as history of exploitation is concerned, it goes back hundreds of years.

When the district of Midnapore was ceded to the British by Mir Qasim in September 1760, it was one of the first districts in India to come under British rule.

You know how the British described them? Hamilton' – an East India Company surgeon, surveyor and botanist – 'as far as I remember said, that these jungles were occupied by a poor miserable proscribed race of men called Santhals. But rebellion lies in the heart of the Santhals and that story goes back as far as medieval times when they resisted the tax collectors.

KB: Honestly, at least in your area of operation, do you think you can sustain this movement for long?

C: Yes, we can sustain it by changing our form of organization. We have to change our form. Our motto will remain the same. We have to change our style of functioning. In the current structure, we cannot survive. We cannot have tribal rights as our only focus when we do have other real issues as well.

But more than tribal rights or intrusive tourism, this abduction is clearly an attempt to buy a ceasefire window from the government that has stepped up the offensive in recent months. This ceasefire provides time to the Maoists to escape and regroup. However, fissures between various Maoist camps have come as a sharp blow. The Andhra Maoists have killed a policeman, almost derailing talks between the Odisha Maoists and the government. The story of Maoist insurgency in India has been one of splits and mergers. But this time it looks ominous for our commander and the rest of the party.

KB: You announced a unilateral ceasefire and appealed to your colleagues operating along the Andhra–Odisha border to abjure violence, but one assistant sub-inspector of police was shot dead. Are there differences within the CPI (Maoist) organization?

C: Yes, there are differences in political views. We think that it is a compulsion for us to take this path since the state is repressive. That's why we take to the gun. But some people are habituated to use the gun, it's a fashion for them. For communists and for revolutionaries, this is an opportunity to function peacefully, apparently peacefully, and they should organize people in a democratic way and in legal struggles. But some people are not interested in this. They only want to take up the gun and move inside the jungles, instead of organizing the vast masses of the people of India. That is the essential difference.

KB: So you are against the armed conflict that many of your other colleagues believe in?

C: Yes, yes, we are ultimately for peace and democracy in our country and the world over. It is the imperialists that wage war and carry out repression. Our reaction is against state repression. I am against unnecessary violence.

KB: [I finally come to the point.] So you will not harm the Italian hostages?

C: If the situation remains like this, and the government doesn't launch offensives against us, I guarantee their safety.

I realize this is the moment to seize and exact something from the man who almost got us killed. Since he maintains such a high moral ground, let's see whether he gives in to the negotiation that is literally on camera. He wants to score over his other colleagues in the Maoist hirerarchy. I just have to convince him that this interview will be broadcast all over and he would then have bargaining power within his party as well in his commanding area. So, I carry on this discussion around his commitment without me having a sausage of an idea of what the government has in mind. But gauging his mind from his smile is tough; he isn't giving away anything. But I will stick to my point. I haven't come here on a picnic. The story will happen anyway, but given the dangers we undertook, let's see how far I can make him stretch.

Then, in what may appear as spontaneous but is certainly a well-thought-out plan, the commander startles me by casually saying he is ready to release one of the hostages unconditionally: 'You can take back one of the hostages. Today we will release one of the hostages and we are also condemning the violence in south Odisha, particularly what our CPI (Maoists) are doing. We are appealing to them to give up violence.'

And just like that, Claudio Colangelo is promised to us. He had been in captivity for ten days. However, we are not allowed to see him yet.

As the sun sets the atmosphere is relaxed, assuming the air of old friends catching up. But where the hostages and the camp are, is still not clear to me. Men and women with guns make their way up and down at regular intervals. A few women can be seen walking down a precarious incline with pots on their head. It is a delicacy prepared in our honour: payasam with cashewnuts. Everybody is getting accustomed to the heat and the flies on the face. The masks have come off and the conversation veers to the 'unfinished revolution'.

The firm but soft-spoken commander argues that the revolution is long dead because the leaders have moved away from ideology to making money and compromises. The commander himself is isolated and under threat from his own colleagues, so he segregates his Odia cadres from the Andhra and Chhattisgarh ones who he suspects have been sent to kill him. He says he opposes any killings and regrets any ambushes his unit has indulged in. He candidly criticizes the policies undertaken by his party, the CPI (Maoist). By now he has repeated several times his opposition to violence. But that has a context. He is accused of assassinating a popular Hindu leader, Swami Laxmanand Saraswati, in Kandhamal district which triggered massive riots. He admits to me it was a mistake.

He continues his rant on the practice of 'unnecessary class annihilations'. 'Beating and burning or eliminating someone by simply stamping him/her as an informer is not the solution.'

The Maoists kill suspected 'informers' regularly to establish their writ. In 2011, an MLA was killed by a Chhattisgarh Maoist squad. The commander had tried to save him, even seeking the help of CCMs (Central Committee members). 'But they never responded and he was simply killed. He was in a wheelchair, a handicapped person.'

'We are too weak in the trade union movement despite our repeated views on this. But we had killed one CITU' – Centre of Indian Trade Unions – 'leader, Thamaso Munda, on the Odisha–Jharkhand border and demolished the trade union office. We can stamp anybody an informer and kill him … without responsibility to convince people of our action! This is our revolutionary birthright! But I mean, why will we demolish the trade union office, the office of common workers?'

The ash from the burning leaves to keep the insects away now settles over us. There is very little activity and most people around us seem too exhausted to react to our conversation. The commander adds a few Bengali words to show his command over languages and to humour me. His disposition is amiable and to our eyes he is the only odd member in his group, perhaps because he is also the only non-tribal.

His biggest grudge against his own party is what he sees as the hegemony of the Telugu-dominated AOB (Andhra–Odisha Border) leadership. 'Our AOB leaders have a superior attitude and have tried to keep the Odisha committee as subordinates ... politically they never think about Odisha, its people's condition and political acceptance.'

It is startling to hear a Maoist commander admit that his own party has degenerated into a feudal democracy, similar to that of the fascist RSS organization.

His anger over the Telugu domination is not over yet. He says that the leadership has forced Telugu food habits on the cadres and has called *pakhal* (an Odia dish) food fit only for the buffaloes. Apparently, the same leader said if cadres don't take mirchi they can't become revolutionaries.

KB: What about financial irregularities?

C: There is not just irregularity but financial anarchy within the party. Many Dandakaranya region cadres in Chhattisgarh are found to be spending as they wish and providing false accounts. Binoy, an area commander, amassed huge wealth before he surrendered and Ashok, another commander, never submitted accounts either.

This is not all. My sectarian comrades are distributing pamphlets against Christianity in Andhra Pradesh's Srikakulam district to strengthen the party's hold on the Sora tribe. As per the new theory of these CCMs, Christianity is the main obstacle to building a revolutionary organization and people's power, and hence we have to target it. Anything discussed at the central committee meetings get leaked.

Though he has been defending tribal rights all day, in the darkest hour of the night he decides to be more honest about his party's policies.

C: We have worked with the tribals for thirty years but the CPI (Maoist) has not developed a concrete model for development of tribal zones. Our *janatana sarkar* (people's government) is not a tribal autonomy body nor is it governed by traditional tribal rules, not even partially ... what type of tribal autonomy do we want to give after the revolution? We have no alternate agricultural, industrial, medical, educational policies.

There is no camp here because the men and women must move every two days, so everything is makeshift. Thin, black plastic sheets that are easy to carry are the bedsheets and the hard earth is the bed. If it rains, well and good, or else it is the malaria-infested, humid air that they breathe. Why would anybody want to live like this and risk their lives for a movement that its leader admits is for all practical purposes dead? What is it that pulls one ethnic group to the movement or is it a stereotype that has been played up again and again? The entire leadership, like the commander himself, is non-tribal but the fighting force is tribal.

C: The Adivasi connection is not unique. If you look through history there have been ethnic/tribal groups, with similar aspirations and grievances who have participated in guerilla wars. In Vietnam, a good number of Viet Minh regulars were Tho tribals. In Kenya, the Mau Mau nationalists were dominated by the Kikuyus. The Kurds challenged the authority in Bahgdad and Tehran. The Karens in Myanmar, the Meos and Yaos in Thailand, and even the Qara, Mahra and Kathir in Arab world. In India, the Nagas and Mizos were at war with the Indian army for decades. Some armed factions are still carrying out military strikes against Indian security forces. You know very well that many more tribal groups in India have been fighting to assert their identity.

The commander is perhaps convincing in his theory but the tribals in the Maoist resistance movement inhabit diverse areas. Who brought them all into one fold? Was it their fierce tradition of independence that made them insurgent against newly established authorities? And in case of Nagas or Mizos or Meiteis (non-tribals) the leaders and cadres of the armed groups have the same ethnicity. In case of Maoists, the leadership is upper-class Hindu whereas the fighting force is from the Adivasi tribals.

KB: So, is there a direct relation between Adivasi history and Naxal mobilization or is it a coincidence?'

C: It may be a coincidence of sorts, but think for yourself about what happened and has been happening, at least in these parts. The tribals will mobilize themselves anyway but without armed resistance they know they will not be able to hold on. See what happened at Kalinganagar[1], Maikanch[2] and Nagarnar[3] – police firing; tribals were killed.

The commander and I stay up to discuss Maoism and tribal resistance history while others are half asleep, sometimes joining in with a comment. One of them is running a high fever and has even thrown up, scaring all of us. The medical corp was prompt to test a blood sample for malaria. None of us have taken anti-malarial drugs, much to the surprise of the commander and his cadres. Once it was established that the test was negative, everyone was administered tablets to immunize us against what seemed like an imminent malaria death trap.

I am curious about the commander's interpretation of the history of Santhal uprising and how the Naxal movement slowly came to be synonymous with Adivasi rights.

KB: Your demands may be legitimate but your means are surely illegal. You can't be terrorizing the population in the name of tribal rights. Show me one village you have decided to set up as a model village. You have enough 'liberated' areas to try and experiment that.

C: When we say tribal rights, you must appreciate the context. Large tracts of Odisha were part of the Madras Presidency[4] that was transformed into excluded/partially excluded areas under the Government of India Act, 1935. No law of the centre or the province was extended to these areas unless so directed by the governor with such modifications, if any. The tribal people in their respective domains managed their affairs according to their custom and tradition. Nobody ever touched this area.

On 26 November 1949, when the constitution was adopted, all the Scheduled Areas automatically came under it. But the governor of the state could direct certain modifications under Para 5(1) of the Fifth Schedule if he felt those were necessary. The irony is that no governor till date has used this power. The governor, and this was clarified in 2011 by the attorney general of India, can amend the laws in their application to the Scheduled Areas without any reference to the state cabinet.

This seemingly minor omission has criminalized the tribals and they can't even enter their own home in the absence of any formal document of which they knew nothing. Earlier, the tribal could settle disputes within his community but suddenly he was told, no, you cannot. To correct these anomalies, PESA [Provisions of Panchayat (Extension to Scheduled Areas) Act], 1996, was passed. Is that being used? No. Amongst our demands, we are saying release people you have detained unfairly and get PESA into action. We are making our demands within the constitutional framework even though we may not believe many things in it. Under PESA, the gram sabhas are the arbitrators.

KB: But isn't that dangerous because these gram sabhas are dictatorial and patriarchal, and can dispense a kangaroo court kind of justice?

C: Do they get any justice outside? Are they fair? And what PESA says is within the constitutional framework so why question it now? We are demanding drinking water, irrigation, health and education – is that illegal? What the government has been denying the tribals is illegal and unacceptable.

KB: You have been repeating the same words over the years and through your gun, but if things are not changing, don't you realize that maybe your methodology is wrong? Maybe you should try something else.

C: The Forest Conservation Act created huge problems for the tribals. You had lakhs of cases by the forest guards against the tribals for collecting even minor forest produce like leaves. Animal conservation meant the priority was animals and the human beings could be dispensed with. But when it suits the government to acquire land for multinationals, then the animals can go to hell.

Resistance against displacement is seen as a law and order problem. What does one do? Not resist? The state has a responsibility under the constitution to protect the tribal people. We are demanding the return of land transferred by fraud. See all our demands and counter me if I have any unreasonable ones. If I am wrong I shall admit it publicly.

KB: So, you are only reiterating what the founding fathers of the constitution, which you don't believe in, had said?

C: You mean the Fifth Schedule of the constitution? Well, that has been torn and thrown away and, yes, we are saying implement that at least. These are known facts: around 80 to 90 per cent of India's mineral wealth, its tropical forests and bulk of its headwaters lie in the heartland of middle and peninsular India and what you all call the 'North East'. Ninety million tribal people live in these ethno-culturally and ecologically sensitive regions. Will you disagree that tribal interests have been hurt through neglect and exploitation? True, the Naxal movement found this a convenient ground to sustain the revolution but what is wrong in that?

KB: You Naxals utilize the terrain the tribals inhabit so while the two are connected, geopolitically didn't it suit your end?

C: That may be your perspective but look back at the history of neglect here. When Tata set up its industry in Jamshedpur, iron ore was sourced from the mountain of Gorumahishani in Mayurbhanj in north Odisha. A complete forest cover was destroyed. Today there are ninety sponge iron factories in north Odisha and over forty new steel plants under construction. Besides environmental damage, it is causing large-scale displacement. How many tribals do you think have been displaced by state policies? It is estimated to be somewhere around twenty million. Way back in the 1920s, a British geologist C.S. Fox had conceived Odisha's big dams and they were meant to supply water and electricity to the plants. Hirakud dam displaced 160,000 people. The resistance was so stiff that it is believed the movement led to the resignation of Odisha's first chief minister. Mandira dam displaced more than 20,000. The list doesn't end here. So you have thrown people out of their homes because it suited you?

Don't forget when the Indian government's Salwa Judum was launched Tata and Essar signed a memorandum of understanding with the government for steel plants. We survive because of these very reasons. Tribals have often resisted in the past but their resistance has been crushed time and again. We support their resistance and give them the confidence to fight.

KB: But you have quietly appropriated this resistance as your own, isn't it?

C: No, we are not there everywhere. Not all tribals are Naxals and this is fundamental, but the tribal cause is something we support. POSCO and Vedanta projects are being resisted. There is resistance in Kalinganagar where 97 per cent of India's chromite deposits are located. In the Kalinganagar movement one policeman was hacked to death and thirteen Adivasis killed in police firing. South Odisha has the world's best quality bauxite depoists and the mountains are held very scared by the Kondh tribe. If you want to demolish those mountains they will resist and we will help them.

Capitalists cannot give up their greed for this natural resource. The Indian government projected an increase in the annual steel production by 40–60 million tonnes to attain a target of 120 million tonnes by 2020. This can only be achieved through mega plants in the coal ore fields of Chhattisgarh, Jharkhand, Odisha and Bengal. All this means deforestation, land acquisition and hill cutting of tribal India.

A Government of India report of 2008 says that in the first forty-five years of Independent India, mining had displaced about two and half crore people and less than a fourth has been rehabilitated. Let me tell you, half of the displaced are Adivasis. For decades now Adivasis have been on the move because of development projects. Do you think it is wrong to point these out?

Now let me come to your Constitution and the Fifth Schedule. I suppose you know that tribal lands cannot be transferred to non-tribals in Fifth Schedule Areas (like the Sixth Schedule in the North East). But the state claims there is an ambiguity whether that applies to government lands. The Samatha judgment of the Supreme Court in 1997 said a lease or land acquisition for public purpose did not entail a transfer. The rich mineral wealth in Scheduled Areas constituted a national asset and the competing rights of tribals and the state were 'required to be adjusted without defeating the rights of either' in the interest of national development. This is very tricky wording. Who will adjust this and decide the balance?

The Fifth Schedule says, the governor of each of these states will make an annual report or whenever the President wants about the administration and then the union government shall advise the state government. The governor is supposed to inquire through the Tribal Advisory Council (TAC).

Has any governor ever used this discretion? No. What, however, happened was that the rules were changed and chief ministers became chairpersons of these councils. Governors were thereby excluded, with the result that the Tribal Advisory Councils have largely become creatures of the chief ministers and state tribal affairs departments. TAC agendas are fixed by the government; the chief minister presides and may include or exclude any item or approve or disapprove anything. So, this part of the Fifth Schedule has been virtually nullified. In fact, these are things I have put forward in my demand and negotiations that are going on right now. Though I am certain that the government won't even look at it but under pressure they may agree and accept. There is nothing in my demand that the government on principle cannot accept.

KB: Well, but you first came to the tribals as friends but like others started to dominate and demand, for example, enrolment of a male and female from each family. You started to levy taxes on cultivation and forest produce and on all government and non-government contracts and infrastructure. How are you different from the state that you are fighting?

C: We are not forcing the tribals and if some of the CPI (Maoist) units are doing that, it is against the revolutionary ideology and I have been vocal about that. Yes, there are accounting frauds, diktats and that's wrong. Agreed. But historical injustice to tribal India was carried out by replacing age-old forest rights by the creation of reserved forests, protected forests, biosphere reserves, buffer zones and the Forest Conservation Act.

Today – that is, 2012 – there are 568 approved SEZs and 315 have been notified and 144 operational. I don't know the latest data. Many more may have been added. The total investment is just short of ₹100,000 crores with exports worth ₹100,000 crores. The land area acquired is close to 2,000 square kilometres, which includes agricultural land and farmland. The contiguity of this land is tribal India and cuts across six states in what you call the 'Maoist corridor'. This corridor is nothing but a stretch of very rich land and people being cheated over centuries. The land belongs to them.

There are Scheduled Areas in nine states, but these exclude some states which have significant tribal populations like Tamil Nadu, Kerala, Karnataka, West Bengal and UP. This is because scheduling is done through the states and not by the President and does not cover all scheduled tribes/tribal belts in the states, only major concentrations, though the Governor can make recommendations for scheduling other areas.

The total tribal population in India is about 100 million, the largest tribal population anywhere in the world, of which about 80 to 85 per cent approximately would be in heartland India, including Fifth Schedule Areas. There are about ten million tribals in the Sixth Schedule Areas located in the northeast region. The two are very different and here we identify the tribes under a common Adivasi term. In reality they are quite distinct from each other but there is a common history of exploitation.

The tribal people of India have struggled for their freedom and rights ever since the British intruded. So, when we date the First War of Independence as having occurred in 1857, we ignore the fact that tribal struggles had gone on for a century before that and continued thereafter. In 1919, when the British instituted constitutional reforms, they declared certain areas to be 'partially' or 'totally' excluded from the civil administration. They were loosely administered by the governors reporting directly to the viceroy.

The Constituent Assembly considered this matter. An advisory committee specially appointed for the purpose felt that exclusion had served little purpose and was not the right answer. Instead, the tribal people needed to be brought into the process of integration and development but not assimilated or steamrolled. So, they felt it necessary to safeguard their identity, livelihoods, customary laws and way of life while helping to promote their development and welfare in accordance with their laws and at their own pace. But that didn't stop them from treating them like exotic zoo animals.

Even the Planning Commission in its report admits that the state has failed. They talked about 'widespread displacement, forest issues, insecure tenancies, and other forms of exploitation like usury, land alienation and imperfect market conditions'.

Isn't it funny that there is a pattern of not implementing the constitutional safeguards but the moment we take it up, the state immediately brings out all the archaic laws to crack down on us?

One of the team members whispers to me that it may be a good idea to stop this argument lest the commander get too worked up. We are entirely at their mercy and they could just take us into their custody as well to put further pressure on the government. If they can arrest two foreigners for virtually no reason, why wouldn't they use us as shields or negotiating tools? I rubbish his fears but all attention is now focused on food. It's dinner time and we are hoping they will not keep us hungry. We may like to believe that we are welcome here, that we are guests, but in reality, we are with a group of armed persons running from the Indian security forces in a hideout where even we could come under attack anytime.

Leaves have again been burned to smoke out the insects and the soldiers are busy with chores in the impenetrable darkness of the night. To the untrained even a step in that darkness makes the feet nervous. Dinner may or may not come. Some of the crew want to go and defecate but where is the water? Jungle life has taught the Maoists to travel light and adapt. The soldiers take out empty plastic pouches of cooking oil neatly folded in their pockets that serve as mugs and quickly go to the water source to fill them up. Boiled drinking water is too precious to wash your backside with. But to find your way to a dignified distance is a challenge. Even after spending a reasonable amount of time in the location, in the darkness the next step seems like the edge of the world. Torchlight is banned for obvious reasons.

Dinner arrives but how does one eat without knowing what one is eating? Fish and chicken have been served but not a piece can be identified. The village apparently donated one chicken but here are some twelve people trying to find its neck and leg. The fish has dissolved into the rice. The adjacent village had apparently gone fishing for the guests but the dinner is not any evidence of that story. But nobody complains here. The commander is in a jovial mood. He has to keep up the morale of the camp every day.

Over dinner we remind the commander that we must return to Daringbari. We had set out saying we would be back in four hours and now it has been two nights already. People must be worried and it hasn't been a pleasant stay at all. But how and when can we return? We are told that nothing can happen at night so the next morning one amongst us will be guided across the mountains to reach the town and get vehicles. However, to assure us, one of the informers carries our cell phones across a mountain to see if he can find the network to send messages to people who have been expecting news from us. The informer returns in one hour without any luck. That one hour would have taken us half a day to traverse.

The crew, save two persons, is in no position to walk any longer. The one with high fever is worrying. Another one has high blood pressure symptoms and a third can barely move his right leg. How will the night pass? More members are falling ill. Two days in the jungle and the entire team is reeling from exhaustion, hunger and heat.

It is decided that the crew will spend the night in the village below because none of the members were willing to sleep on thin plastic sheets with millions of insects and mosquitoes hovering around. A woman deputy slings her gun across her shoulders and briskly leads the team down a slope to a village house where the inmates are forced to vacate the verandah where the crew is to sleep. There was a mild resistance or perhaps an inquiry, but she is in command and means business. The authority with which she is speaking is evidence of her power over them, possibly through threat of the gun. It isn't pleasant to displace the owners and push them inside their rooms when they were enjoying the cool breeze outside.

There is a breeze now, probably from the stream flowing by, and the weariness of two days overwhelms the crew. The last cigarette smoked, there is nothing now left to distract us. Sleep comes and goes like a periodic dream and nightmare. Everyone is uncomfortable but the body needs rest. The surface is hard and mud baked and there is nothing to cover the bodies. On one side is a bamboo wall and the other a human body. Legs stick out because the verandah is rather small. If there was some activity around one could have even sat through the night. But this is a different world. It is dispossessed, poor, disconnected and fearful. Nobody speaks to outsiders here. They don't even show themselves. They know the police will come tomorrow and interrogate them, even harass and probably abuse. This will ensure a few more boys and girls join this army. The village caught in this crossfire is like an absent row of houses stubbornly and silently refusing to participate in the story of the world's largest democracy.

A hundred thoughts run through the mind in slo-mo. Is sleep only a bodily function? I left behind a phone that may be ringing. I haven't informed anyone about this adventure so surely some people must be worrying about our safety. Perhaps nobody has called knowing that cell phone or landline phone connectivity is poor at our base camp.

But the biggest concern now is how to get out of here. Walking back the same route is not an option. The majority of the crew won't make it. It has been a really bad decision but getting one of the hostages released is a huge breakthrough. The other concern is whether it is prudent to take him back. If something happens to him we would be held responsible. At the same time, one cannot leave him behind. The reason for undertaking this arduous journey was to film the story of the 'hostage crisis' and not to negotiate for their release. But the police was discreetly informed not to follow us so that we can assess the situation. Whether the commander knows it or not, his movements are now being tracked by the government forces and if it weren't for the lives of the two hostages being at risk, an operation would have been launched. But nothing was officially communicated about the security forces refraining from an attack at this time; we just have to keep trusting the cops. What is odd, however, is that we haven't even seen the hostages yet.

25 March 2012

With barely any sleep everyone is up before dawn but there is little to do. The villagers are so impoverished that even a cup of tea is not available. One house has lit a fire to cook the day's meal but there is nothing besides rice in the kitchen. I sit near the fire to have a conversation with our hosts. But they have very little to share or even complain about. There is weariness in their eyes and resignation in their voices. They are certainly not participants of any revolution.

With the return to Daringbari scheduled for today, only two of us are fit to undertake the journey to bring back reinforcements to take back one of the hostages and the crew. They, of course, haven't revealed how that would be made possible. My stamina is on its last lap but I must make it or else we are doomed. Guided by two villagers one has to scale a high mountain, rocky and steep. I decide to invent my own climbing technique of counting ten steps and pausing. Two nights of sleeplessness, several hours of trekking, hunger, uncertainty and helplessness are making it tough to even force myself to go forward.

This hill path must be an old inhabited part of Kandhamal. It has ancient temples on its way and there is some movement of people. It is early morning and the villagers are collecting toddy from date trees. They offer us fresh toddy that is supposed to give strength and on an empty stomach, that seems like a good option. A drinking jar made of gourd is filled with the drink and we are given generous helpings of the morning's collection. We settle down on a huge rock and exchange pleasantries. A dog follows us and settles on another rock. Nobody is curious to know what are we doing in this village. Intoxication is a part of the tribal life here; in other parts the brew is made of mohua flowers. Farmers and hunters carry their brew made of fermented millet to keep them going through the day. Every household ferments and consumes alcohol. It is a part of the daily diet.

As I count ten steps and stop to catch my breath, the hill seems endless. Finally, it opens up to a plateau and a village with some men playing volleyball. It is a large village with shops and schools and a church. The drinking water facility where I spend a long time under the tap has been donated by some Christian missionary organization. Tea and biscuits from the village shop serve as breakfast while the guides negotiate to hire a motorcycle to ferry us to the town.

It is like freedom for us after what seemed an endless detention. It didn't take us very long though the climb must have been a couple of thousand feet. Here, life suddenly seems normal. We feel dazed and sit in someone's house, trying to come to terms with the fact that the rest of the world has been moving on just the way we had left it behind. How strange – two days of a jungle trek and some unusual experiences make this 'normal' atmosphere almost unreal. It was just two days for us while the militia spend all their lives moving from one part of the jungle to another till they are killed, arrested or they surrender. There are no other options. Usurpation of power is not something that will happen and they are acutely aware of it. But one doubts whether they suffer from the dilemma to continue or not. Life otherwise is miserable so this seems to some a reasonable option. Personal experiences help in the radicalization. The others are sympathetic and lend support while many go about their own lives indifferent to any hope the party offers.

We cannot be identified as the police may trail us back, despite assurances, and now we must call our vehicle, without giving away news of our return, to go and fetch the rest of the crew and the hostage. Since there was no news of us for two days, the town was abuzz with rumours that we may have been abducted as well. The cell phones barely work here but after several attempts, we manage to contact the vehicle driver. We decide on a particular point to meet the vehicle and proceed towards it. It has to be outside the town limits and nobody can get wind of our arrival because that would jeopardize Claudio's release.

Finally, a motorbike is arranged for a few hundred rupees to drop us to the town. Energized with the feeling of freedom, we make our way through impossible roads but stunning landscape. Our only thought now is not to be identified by anyone. Our prolonged stay at Daringbari has made us familiar to a lot of people. The motorbike moves away from the main road to a dirt track to avoid curious eyes and at the given point we meet our two designated vehicles. As we transfer ourselves into the vehicles we are spotted by a vehicle from another TV network. They ignore our presence. The life of one hostage is now entirely in our hands and we can carry out our 'mission' only if we can sneak out unnoticed to another unknown destination. We have not been told anything specific but given only a lead. Guerillas never tell you the details. And though the police have been told to leave us alone, that is not a guarantee.

Partly on intuition and partly common sense we head towards a reserve forest from where we are told a village road on our right enters the forest. With nobody to guide us, the drivers take it upon themselves to find the way. From the forested road, suddenly a bicycle crosses us from the opposite direction indicating that we move ahead. I vaguely note that the rider in plain clothes was the same one who had served us lunch the previous day. They can merge with the local population and that is the strength of this militia.

The drivers are subtly signalled to stop at a shop selling cheap cigarettes and biscuits by a well with a shading tree nearby. The bicycle rider moves ahead to check whether we are being followed and so we try to relax in the shade. The energy threshold has broken but we are too close to give up. The rest of the crew is waiting and this operation must be carried out swiftly. The big vehicles would have left a trail and it is not unlikely that someone may have followed us. It takes a while for our man to return with an all-clear signal and the daily stock for his colleagues. It's irritating to say the least. There is no revolution happening here. No lives are changing. And these delays and cloak-and-dagger scenarios have become very trying.

The supplies for the camp inmates are stuffed into our vehicles. This is a safe zone, so the guide leaves his bicycle and joins us. He looks much older than his age. The commander had narrated his story to us the previous evening. He was made to witness his sister get raped and killed by security forces because his brother had joined the underground movement and the family was harassed and abused. After his brother's death in an encounter he too joined but would spend most of his free time worrying and in a year's time he started ageing. He can never get over the sight of his sister's sexual assault. He doesn't talk much but he smiles all the time.

Road posts to guide us have already been set up along a precarious track passing through streams and forests. The destination seems closer than I imagined. It feels foolish to be now driving to the camp when we were made to undergo a cross-country endurance test earlier. The sixteen-hour trek was just to avoid the police and confuse us. This camp could have been reached in one hour by vehicle.

Meanwhile Claudio is still in the makeshift camp counting the hours, hoping it is going to be freedom at last!

As our two vehicles make their way through rivulets and by felled trees the landscape looks familiar. I recognize the village where we had slept the previous evening. From what now looks like a natural hideout we see the rest of the crew along with Claudio walking towards us. None of the cadres are accompanying them.

Wearing a round-necked T-shirt, water-resistant cargo trousers and waterproof caterpillar boots and carrying a stick, Claudio looks angry but relieved as he moves forward. Of medium height and average build, his face is taut and he can barely smile. There is the natural anger of having been imprisoned for ten days for no good reason. He is tired of it all and can barely wait to get out but he is cautious of his surroundings and the people he is now reposing faith on.

The vehicles must now find their own way back with no more contact with the guides. The camp has to be dismantled immediately and the entire brigade has to move to a new location to avoid detection.

Though we simply need to retrace the track we took to get here, the return is difficult. There are no guides with us and the vehicles are finding it difficult to manoeuvre through the gradients. While crossing a stream across the track we get stuck for a while and the worry is sudden identification by the security forces engaged in operations. Claudio too gets off the vehicle to join us negotiate an uphill operation with a stream overflowing the road. With great difficulty we manage to get the vehicles moving but the collective sense of relief and excitement is enough get past any hitch right now.

Suddenly, in the middle of the forest where there is no network, the cell phone rings. We stop to pass on the news of the release. Claudio is connected to the outside world where he himself announces his freedom. He will have to wait for some more time to be able to speak to his family.

At the first police outpost, Claudio is handed over. It's a job well done, though until this morning, it had seemed impossible.

PART II

Claudio Colangelo is a sixty-one-year-old Italian and this is his third visit to India. He came across Paolo Bosusco while searching the Internet for ways to visit tribal areas in India. Claudio has an enduring interest in ethnicity and travels the world to live in tribal areas and study tribes. His original plan was to visit the north-eastern part of India but due to technical difficulties he chose Odisha.

For two years I have been looking forward to visiting the tribal areas of Assam, Arunachal Pradesh and Nagaland but the Protected Area Permit restrictions – the act requires travelling in groups – made me change my mind. While browsing the Internet, I found Paolo's website that provided very interesting information about Odisha tribes and his interest in trekking the tribal terrain. Once I got in touch with Paolo by mail, I told him I was going to join him as soon as possible and that's how I came to be in Odisha.

I land in Bhubaneswar late evening on 11 March 2012. The heat and the odour of India hit my senses, reminding me of my earlier visits.

The last time I visited this country was almost thirty-five years ago when I was in Rajasthan with my wife Silvana, but the wonderful experience I had at that time had never left me. And the first time was a brief stopover in Bombay while returning home from our honeymoon in Thailand.

April 1974

I recall the impact was very strong. A wave of heat and smells assaulted me as I went down the aircraft steps. The building of the airport was rather modest and lacked air conditioning. Visa procedures occurred at an excruciatingly slow pace, but our attention was claimed by the people around in long white kurtas with their serene tanned faces. Outside, I was struck by the colourful turbans and the earthy smells. I think it was the smells that dominated our first encounter with India.

The trip by taxi to the Taj Mahal Hotel revealed an incredible world. Innumerable people sleeping on the street and hundreds of crows flying all over foraging for food. People urinating and defecating on the roadside. A woman of uncertain age begging at the traffic lights with a child desperately trying to suck milk from her breast that probably had none. It was miserable but this poverty, this suffering, failed to shut our eyes to the charm of this new world. There is something in the air of this country that spells hope and makes you believe in miracles.

We arrived at the Taj Mahal Hotel where we were welcomed by the glamour of another India, the rich India. We went strolling on the roads of Bombay, starting from the Gateway of India and moving to the incredible shopping streets, a display of glittering products. Hundreds of rickshaws were trying to attract our attention. At traffic intersections, slum kids were trying to sell us a variety of stuff to earn their meal for the day. Myriads of colours shone from the products on display in stores – strong colours that blended into a beautiful mélange. So much vitality, so much noise. The five days ended too soon.

We had to go back home with a promise that we would come back again.

March 1978

We were back in Delhi to keep our promise. This time we were more prepared and looking forward to absorbing the sounds and smells, enjoying this wonderful country and her marvellous people.

Our trip had been well detailed in advance – we were to visit Agra, Jaipur, Udaipur, then head to Khajuraho and Benares (as it used to be called at that time).

The rich colours of Jaipur and the deep sense of love embedded in the Taj Mahal in Agra filled our souls. We fell deeply in love with this country that began to feel more and more ours. What a magical place this was. Deprivation, squalor, poverty but amidst all these, the soul of a nation, a people, throbs every moment even at the burning ghats of Benares where one celebrates death. India is not exotic as the West tends to think of it; it is deeply philosophical and stirs you from within. There are many Indias at every level and there are multiple levels and you can choose where you want to be, what you want to see and how you want to see this country. It would take us many lifetimes to really experience this place.

We enjoyed the charm of the lake hotel in Udaipur, a heritage mansion. And what luck to be in Khajuraho during Holi, probably the most colourful festival ever. The waves of gulal against the ancient ruins of a continuing civilization are mesmerizing for an outsider. We were totally taken in by the intoxication of India.

But it was in Benares, I think, that I became a true Indian. It was here I felt that spiritual connect between the soul and the body and the people around as one humanity. India is here. One of the oldest cities of the world, here the river and the temple bells, the cows and the pilgrims, the ascetics and the chants merge and create an aura of divinity. It is not a sense and a feeling another city can offer. It must have acquired this after centuries of meditation along the banks of the Ganga flowing from the Himalayas. The beauty of Benares is a felt experience, not something I can describe. We sat by the river and saw hundreds of devotees take the holy dip meant to cleanse them of their sins and purify their souls. It is a city of faith and faith can move mountains, they say.

Many years after that soul-enriching trip I am finally back in India but what a situation I have managed to get myself in!

11 March 2012

After landing in Bhubaneswar, I try to get a taxi to Puri but the price I am quoted is far beyond my budget, so I start looking for a rickshaw to the downtown bus stop.

After twenty minutes of waiting, during which not even a tuk-tuk passed, I spot a young man on the sidewalk. I ask him where I could find a cheap means of transport to get to the bus stop heading to Puri. With a broad smile he tells me he is going to Puri and, if I'm fine with it, he could give me a lift. His relatives are coming to pick him up in a while, in a car.

Bhubaneswar to an average Indian may be an idea of a planned city but to me it is rather confusing. I suppose any Indian city can be confusing and sometimes that is part of the charm to an outsider. The road signs can easily misdirect even the city resident. Though some may find the people on the road either overbearing or rude, I see the attitude as an interesting facet of this fascinating country. They may appear suspicious to the inexperienced but I can boast of a fair share of Indian experiences that have taught me not to be so wary. Some people stalk and harass western tourists or dupe them. India is very far from being sensitized about how to behave with foreign tourists but I can manage rather well. (Or so I thought.) In every western tourist, many people sense a potential prey. Though anyone visiting India is aware of this ugly welcome ritual, it can be very irritating and even unsafe for most.

Not even thinking for a second of the possible danger in going with a foreigner in a strange environment, I accept the young man's offer with the condition that I would pay him ₹400, a sum I was ready to pay for a taxi.

The deal is done and in a while I am in a jeep, among five Indians speaking the local language, along a dark road. The Indian family is headed, as I understand, for the coastal town of Puri to visit the famous Jagannath temple. We arrive in Puri late in the night.

It is not possible to experience India without religion and antiquity. But religion is not something that excites me. To the average foreigner Indian shrines are a huge draw. Puri is full of temples and the Jagannath temple is one of the holiest shrines of the Hindus, I am told. The three idols in the temple, Jagannath, Balabhadra and Shubhadra, have been in Indian civilization for a very long time. Their appearance to me is somewhat android with big dark shades on their eyes. They are supposed to be manifestations of the omnipresent, omniscient and omnipotent. I did some homework before I arrived this time in India! These statues are made of the wood of the neem tree while the other statues in the temple are carved out of stone. These wooden gods are renewed every nineteen years during the double Asadha (June–July) through a secret ritual, *nabakalebara*.

I have seen one of the finest pieces of historical documentation of the Puri Jagannath temple – the Copenhagen Yatripata of Puri kept in the Danish National Museum at Copenhagen. The painting was a 'political gift' in 1827 by the raja of Khurda or Puri to F. Mansbach, a Danish national working for the East India Company as a sub collector in Puri.[1] All this is intriguing to me but the intention behind this visit is certainly not the temple. My enduring interest has been tribal life and community.

Therefore, what interests me most of all about the Jagannath temple is that the origins of the temple are largely speculative but are believed to have tribal connections. Since no non-Hindus are allowed inside the temple most of the western accounts fail to describe the iconography. Initially General Cunningham, often regarded as the 'father of Indian archaeology', suggested that the temple was built on a Buddhist shrine and the idols therefore resemble the Buddhist symbol of Triratna. There were many other reasons for believing in the Buddhist connection including the no-caste barrier in the temple.[2] But with time the Buddhist theory has been challenged. Some believe it may have been a Tantric temple dedicated to the worship of Brahma, Vishnu and Shiva as well as the three aspects of Shakti.

Verrier Elwin, who is supposed to be the authority on tribes and ethnography in India and who I have read only a little, claimed that the Daitas and the Suars, the non-Brahmin attendants and cooks in the Jagannath temple, are descendants of the Sora tribe or Saoras[3]. He has an interesting description of the Daitas who are apparently responsible for identifying the new trees from which the idols are remade and how they observe mourning for the old idols like they would if someone died in their clan. The image of Jagannath in the curiously stunted form looks as if it might have come down from the Ganjam Hills. He finds resemblance to Kittung, the Sora tribal god, and the shape of a log of wood out of which these idols are fashioned are also gods of the Murias and Maria Gonds. Legends seem to suggest that the rulers of the region realized they couldn't rule without recognizing the tribal gods of the area. Does the Jagannath temple iconography indicate Hinduisation of the tribal gods?

I must admit that all this is very new to me about India. I had visited the north and the west but this is my first eastern sojourn. Odisha has various art forms, as I could see. Kalahandi, for example, has a dance and music form like Ghoomra, Koraput produces the famous Kotpad natural colour sarees and Bolangir weaves the Bomkai saree. The essence of India is pretty much here, from Gitagovinda to Jayadeva's love lyrics, from the sculptures of Konark and Bhubaneswar to the Patachitras and from Dalkhai Adivasi dance tradition to the Odisi Nritya. It is an ancient region with a very rich history, where tribals have lived for centuries – and about whom other Indians know so little. But this time I have little time for heritage, I want to head for the forests right away.

The sound of the sea can be heard and with the turn to the beachfront the high waves and saline air reassure me. It is a beautiful beach with high waves but I can't spot a single person in beachwear. Instead they are in semi-formal dress, as if taking a stroll in their own locality. Some women are dressed in nightwear, the men in boxer shorts. Most of them are speaking loudly, probably discussing food. There are rows of fast food stalls selling various kinds of fried snacks; hawkers shout in a bid to attract customers. Rickshaws clank away at great speed through the milling crowd. Photographers woo customers. The entire stretch is dotted with beggars and pilgrims. I don't even have the interest to take out my camera for some shots. Besides, it is too dark.

Following my guide Paolo's suggestion, I spend the night at a lodge next to his office. The room is very shabby; there is no air conditioning and the toilet quite dirty, but I am so looking forward to my trip to the forest that I don't want to waste any time searching for another hotel. I throw my belongings on the bed and step out to meet Paolo in a nearby restaurant.

Puri is littered with hotels and inns of all prices, including very expensive luxury hotels. But the beachfront which runs along the town limits has an ugly façade of unattractive hotels. This beach, I am told, is usually populated with tourists from the neighbouring state of West Bengal. Pilgrimage tourism is what is popular here. I learn that beachwear is hardly visible because the conservative middle-class Bengali crowd is unlikely to be sunbathing or indulging in watersports. But it is a happy place with lots of sounds and a carnival-like atmosphere even at this time of the evening.

The first impression I get of Paolo is of a free-spirited man who does not conform to the 'common life' expectations. Very long blond hair, skinny, relaxed and very talkative. I like him. He seems to know so much about ethnic groups and not just about India but from across the world. We exchange our views on the subject and the more we talk, the more confident I feel about him.

But there is some bad news waiting for me. Paolo reveals that just a few weeks ago, the Odisha government banned tourism in most of the tribal areas. But all is not lost as it were; there is a possibility of visiting an area not considered 'tribal' where we will have the opportunity to come in contact with Kui Kondh tribals, where he has many friends among the locals.

For such a long time I have been dreaming about this trip and the diversities I would experience, and now this … Well, I have to accept cutting down the plan of twenty days of trekking in the northern part of the state into a five-day trek in the southern part.

Two days later, at five o' clock in the morning, I am in a jeep heading to Daringbari, with Paolo, my Italian guide, and two locals – a cook and a porter.

After a very slow and long trip we arrived in Daringibari. The road from Bhubaneswar passes by Chilka Lake where seafood is the specialty. But not all the food stalls serve quality seafood. After hours of plain land with rocky mountains on either side, the road slowly meanders by ghats and ancient temples to this unique pine tree valley where it apparently snows in the winter. I must cross-check this fact because it sounds quite bizarre that it can snow in this area.

We get off the car to stretch our legs. It is a very small town and very unlike Bhubaneswar or Puri. The street is crowded and noisy. Some buses pass by with lots of people sitting on the roof. Even in such a remote village the road traffic is chaotic. The few cars and buses try to make their way between the carts and pedestrians, honking interminably.

Paolo stops at a little vegetable stall to buy some provisions for the trek. People look at us with interest. I guess two 'whites' in these parts are a rarity. I answer with a smile to their looks and they immediately reciprocate. We then go for lunch to a place that is supposed to be a 'restaurant' but whose hygiene leaves much to be desired. But this is no time to be squeamish –

we have some scrambled eggs and undefined cooked vegetables of undefined taste. After the quick lunch, we go to the police station to seek permission to go into the jungle. We take note of the police officer's name and telephone number and get on with our five-day trek.

14 March 2012

We wake up at first light. One more night in the jungle and then we head back. I hope that on the 16th we will be in a place where there is phone network. I want to call Silvana for our thirty-eighth wedding anniversary.

We spend some more time with a tribal family. They are preparing a pile of mud and dung bricks for cooking fuel. By eleven o' clock we start our walk, moving along the course of a river. It is a hot day. At one point, we pass a local school where the students sit on the dirt listening to the teacher. Despite the wretched condition of the 'classroom', every student is attentive and in uniform.

In a couple of hours, we settle our camp on the riverbank and the cook begins the preparations for lunch. I am very exhausted after the walk so I decide to jump in the river to have a bath and to wash my trousers that, after three days, definitely need a wash. Half naked, I walk between the big rocks in the middle of the riverbed, looking for deep enough water. Paolo takes a bath as well.

After twenty minutes we are back at the camp, ready for lunch. I am looking at the cook, wondering when the food will be ready, when four armed men emerge from the green of the forest pointing their guns at us. They are wearing Castro-style hats with red stars. I am the first one to realize what's going on and I raise my arms, indicating surrender. I call out to Paolo to alert him. The gunmen shout, asking us to lie on the ground, while Paolo tries to speak to them in the local dialect.

'Shut up!'

This is the only thing they say, kicking him in the ass. Paolo keeps asking to talk with their commander but the only answer is more kicks. I also get kicked because I am not yet on the ground. They start yelling, 'Pistols! Pistols!' We tell them we have no weapons. Then everybody goes quiet. They ask me to put my arms behind my back, then tie my wrists so tightly that it hurts. I sense they are looking into our backpacks but I cannot see them because I am not allowed to lift my head. It looks like they know exactly what to do. From the noises I am able to hear, I realize that some of the people who were around us were leaving the place. Have they left us then?

After some time they command us to stand up and start crossing the river. I realize that our backpacks have been taken away. I tell Paolo to request them to let me get my trousers that are drying on a rock in the middle of the riverbed, and they agree.

Once on the other side of the river, we are blindfolded and with hands tied behind the back, we are made to walk towards the top of the hill. I am still not feeling scared but am dying to know exactly who these fellows are. Are they communists or are they bandits? The latter may be more dangerous. Very likely they are Naxalites. Paolo had told me this area is their territory, but he also told me they are not interested in tourists; they are fighting against the local administration and the Indian government. They are extreme left-wing groups who have been around for a very long time.

I haven't done anything wrong to them. If they are Naxalites, they will release us immediately, I assure myself.

Climbing the side of a mountain blindfolded and with hands tied behind your back is a very tough business. Luckily someone is holding me under one arm; nevertheless, more than once I lose my balance and fall, bumping my shins on roots or branches, and I am injured. From the noise of the footsteps, I can make out that the others are coming up with me. Well, maybe they will not separate us.

The climb seems endless. All the muscles are in constant tension, not knowing how and where to find support for walking. The rope on the wrist becomes increasingly painful and I ask Paolo to request if they can loosen it up a little. That request is immediately rejected.

I have lost all track of time. We arrive at a place where some other people seem to be waiting for us. Finally, I can sit down. For a few minutes I only listen to the noises around me. Then suddenly a very calm voice starts talking to me in English with a rather good accent.

'What's your name?' I am asked first.

As calm as I have been up to now, I start answering lots of questions about nationality, address, work, income (here I lie, understating it because I wouldn't like them to eye my money), reason for my visit, whether I know where I am and so on. It goes on and on, and it is irritating me rather than scaring me.

By the way the questions are posed, I understand I am among a structured military-style setup. If they had been bandits, they wouldn't be so specific in their questions.

I do not feel distressed at all. I am sure they will understand they are making a mistake. I have nothing to do with their fight with the Indian state.

Suddenly they remove the blindfold.

No, no, I don't like what I see around me. Yes, it is a militia but if they are not afraid to be recognized, maybe they will kill us sooner or later. I look around at the armed people. Surprisingly, they are all teenagers, at least the ones in my sight. All are silent, dressed in improvised uniforms and light rubber shoes.

I see a man with a moustache, wearing a military uniform. His expression is not aggressive; it reflects the calmness with which he asks me the questions.

'What do you want from me?' I ask. 'I will tell you later,' he says as he keeps asking questions, very sharp in his interrogation.

Around me I can see a few other young armed guys in uniform, but I don't want to look around too much. The less I know, the better it is. While I am answering, somebody at my back unties the rope around my wrists. What a relief!

'Okay, that's enough, you can sit there,' the man says to me, pointing to a yellow tarp lying about fifty feet below where we were. 'Now we are going to question your friends,' he says, gesturing to my right, where I see Paolo and the others sitting on the ground, still blindfolded and with hands tied behind their back. Some armed soldiers are watching them very closely. 'If you have lied to me, you will be in trouble.'

Once more, I don't feel threatened, only hoping Paolo and the others tell the truth.

It feels unreal to me. What are we doing here? Don't they understand they made a mistake? Is it not clear enough that I am an Italian? As my mind whirls with questions I head for the site they prepared to keep us clean. Yes, to keep us clean while all around us the forest is burned and the ground is full of ash. That's very kind of them but maybe it's a must: you must stay as clean as possible if you are short of water and I don't see any water around us.

I sit on the yellow tarp. It's almost nine by nine square feet and has been placed over a horizontal platform along the steep slope of the hill. These people know how to make their environment livable.

While I hear unintelligible chattering from the back, I keep looking around me. One hundred and fifty feet further down I see our backpacks watched over by a sentry. I don't know why but this looks good to me. After a while, one at a time, my two Indians trek mates join me. No one utters a word.

Our eyes are fixed in front of us but I spot tears rolling down the cheeks of our cook. 'Don't worry,' I say, 'they'll let us go.' But I am not fully convinced myself.

After another half an hour, Paolo finally comes and sits with us on the yellow tarp. We exchange notes and agree that we are in the hands of the Naxalites I had heard about. Not a big discovery but it's something to start from.

Paolo tells me he has asked the commander to release everybody and keep him as hostage. That's very kind of him but I doubt they'll do this. If they want to utilize us for some kind of negotiation, they wouldn't release somebody for free. Finally, we agree to avoid any action or behaviour that could endanger ours or somebody else's life.

We are not so eager to talk and we are also extremely tired. The slope of the hill was very steep and we have not even had lunch. It is now late afternoon and the light is getting increasingly weak. I also have a little cold. Perhaps it is general weakness or maybe the end of the adrenaline charge. Through Paolo, I ask the sentinel if I can take out the jacket that is in my small backpack, sitting by our pile of luggage. The sentinel asks the commander who immediately agrees. Well, at least they don't want us to suffer unnecessarily.

My small backpack is given to me. Opening the zip I realize some cash I had in the backpack is still there; despite them frisking our belongings, the valuables are as they were. It is almost €300, a considerable amount for them, and it's impossible that they didn't see it – it is lying on top, the first thing one sees when opening the zip. This gives me a very positive picture of the commander's men. They are not looking for money. But my biggest surprise is to find my iPhone at the bottom of the backpack.

The phone is off and they may not have recognized it as a phone. Perhaps at night I could try to send a message to warn about the abduction; but will there be any network? I wish I had my new friend Salman's signal booster. And what if they discover me sending a message? I may put the others and myself in a very difficult situation.

I show Paolo my iPhone and he suggests avoiding using it. I think he is right.

Exhausted after the very stressful day, we eat some crackers and chocolate from our food supply and lie down, trying to fall asleep. It's the first time in my life that I am sleeping in the open in the middle of a jungle. I stare at the tops of trees and the stars peeping through the leaves. My thoughts turn to my wife and my children. I cringe, thinking of the pain they will feel when they learn of my abduction, the panic and fear they will be subjected to as they contemplate scenes of brutal violence associated with such abductions. They will feel helpless. But why am I conjuring up such images? Is it some kind of a pleasure to imagine how my near ones will react when I am in trouble?

Oh God, why did I do this to them? Why, for my thrill of these adventurous journeys, do they have to suffer so much?

This thought becomes an obsessive refrain in my mind. At a certain point in time, I start feeling cold. I ask Paolo to talk to the sentries to see if we are allowed to take out the sleeping bags in our backpacks. The minute he mentions it the commander orders his men to bring the backpacks to us.

I appreciate how gentle they are being with us at the moment and then I fall asleep, exhausted, in the warmth of my sleeping bag.

I wake up at dawn. Our jailers are already in motion, like laborious ants. My mates are waking up as well. The air is nice and fresh. If I were not in this position, this would be an idyllic situation. But the firearms all around bring me back to reality. Our cook is allowed to make us some tea for breakfast. We swallow it in a rush and start moving.

With the excuse that I'm old, I refuse to carry my backpack. I want to give them a sense that for them I will be a burden. While a patrol of four or five soldiers goes in one direction, we start to move in the opposite one. Just after half an hour of walking, we enter into deeper jungle and the commander orders us to squat.

Now, in the plain light of the morning and with a clear head, I start observing my captors. Apart from the commander who is about forty-five or fifty years old, the others are young men and women. Some of the girls cannot be older than fifteen. All have a very professional expression but they do not show aggressive behaviour towards us. Everybody is very quiet; if they talk to each other, they do it in whispers.

After about an hour of waiting, sitting on the hill, my mind again goes back to ruminate on the likely suffering of my family and tears well up in my eyes. I try to hide this little weakness, not because I am ashamed but because I would not give them the satisfaction of seeing me scared or vulnerable. But many eyes are on us just to make sure we do not try to escape.

'Why are you crying?' says the commander.

'Guess,' I say to him. 'By tomorrow my family expects a phone call from me and if they don't receive any news, they will get anxious. They will probably discover I have been kidnapped and they will feel desperate, and it's all because of my stupid desire for adventurous trips. I feel terribly guilty and worried about my wife. She can have a heart attack.'

'You shouldn't worry,' says the commander. 'We are not like the police, and we are not heartless. How long would you be able to cooperate?'

At these simple words, my mind lightens. This is not an insensitive man. Probably he only wants to use us as a means of negotiation.

'You cannot ask me to cooperate,' I say. 'This is not my war. It's your war. If you want, you can keep me in custody as long as you like, I cannot avoid it; but if you allow me to go, I will leave immediately.'

I say that very impulsively; maybe I should have showed a little more diplomacy. But there is anger in me and the desperate situation makes me impulsive. What is he even thinking? Recruiting us as his agents? He may be better than other such people we read about but what kind of ridiculous talk is this!

But after this exchange of words, I actually feel much relieved. His behaviour and his statements don't give me a bad feeling, but I have to make the best use of this information. As the commander seems to be a sensitive person, I should exploit this 'weakness'.

I decide to reinforce the impression that I'm an old, weak man. I will act almost depressed, worried sick about my family and the situation. Maybe in the long run this may influence the commander's 'soft heart'.

After almost four hours of squatting in the bush, the patrol comes back and exchanges some information with the commander. Very likely they didn't find any trouble around because we start moving leisurely and, after a further half an hour walk, we are shown our new camp.

How on earth did I land myself in the middle of this war? Silvana, I am sorry, I am really sorry.

15 March 2012

It is about ten in the morning and the temperature is soaring. Soldiers set up for us a small pad that is sufficiently even to sit comfortably. With a heavy crowbar they first remove the stones that would make it unbearable to sit. It's amazing how efficient and organized they are. Everyone knows exactly what to do and performs their tasks in silence, seemingly without effort. One of the girls uses a light blanket to create a sort of canopy to shade the spot where the commander sits. We sit on a tarp covering the flat section created specifically for us. Nobody bothers us. We are allowed to stand up and walk around within the limits of the area guarded by sentries.

I am not clear how many soldiers there are around. My inability to remember the faces prevents me from having a clear idea of the numbers. Logically, I suppose there are more placed further in the distance who we can't see. No one speaks to us but two or three soldiers are always sitting very close to us.

When the commander talks to a soldier, the others seem to know exactly what to do. Any activity they conduct, they always carry a weapon on their shoulder.

I start talking to Paolo to see if he has a better idea than me about the number of armed personnel strolling around, but he doesn't seem to. Paolo goes to the commander and starts talking to him in Odia.

Damn, I would like to be able to understand the local language! It would be much easier if I understood what was going on. Fortunately the commander speaks perfect English; I will grab a chance to talk to him. He seems to be a cultured person and educated too.

When Paolo comes back, he tells me that the commander hasn't said anything specific about our prospects. Paolo says that kidnapping of local administrators by the Naxalites is quite usual; normally negotiations with the government start very soon and they arrive at a solution within a fortnight. He has never heard about the involvement of foreigners in such affairs. To be honest, I am not very proud to be the first kidnapped foreigner, and I don't give a shit about their negotiations. I have nothing to do with their war. I am really pissed off. They are causing my family such distress for their own objectives. I don't really feel personally threatened but the idea of my loved ones suffering because of me, with the lack of news about my fate, sends me into a tizzy.

It's been a couple of hours since we camped but my restlessness is making me more and more edgy. I finally decide to approach the commander.

Claudio Colangelo (CC): Commander, I would like to express my appreciation for your cadres. When they searched in my backpack, despite finding a good amount of cash, they didn't touch it.

C: [very calmly]: We have more money than you could ever have.

What a statement. I believe that the commander is a very proud man. But let's go on.

CC: Why did you abduct us? What have we done wrong?

C: You have been going into a forbidden area clicking pictures of tribal women as if they are exotic zoo animals.

CC: But forbidden by who? The government didn't declare this area forbidden to foreigners. And the tribals don't have a problem being photographed. And everywhere in the world ethnography is a subject that is documented, and how will you document without pictures?

C: This is a tribal area and we, the Naxalites, have declared all tribal areas forbidden to outsiders, whoever they are.

CC: But how would I know that? If anybody in the morning wakes up and establishes a new forbidden area on his own, that's going to be impossible to manage. It would be chaos, a kind of anarchy.

C: It is your duty to inform yourself on local customs. We want to protect the tribals from outside influences.

CC: But this is just ridiculous. How can I inform myself, from Italy, about a local edict issued by a paramilitary organization, of course not officially recognized?

C: You may not know, but your guide should know it.

At this sentence I cannot argue any more.

CC: But what do you want to do with us?

C: I will let you know soon.

And he goes to his soldiers. There hasn't been a real answer to my questions, and all of it sound to me more like justifications than genuine reasons, but at least he seems to be willing to exchange opinions and doesn't overreact when challenged.

The day passes slowly without any further exchange of words with the commander. The heat is oppressive and we can take shelter from the sun only between the branches that survived the burning of the forest.

So our fault was clicking pictures? That's all?

•

I remember the day we set out on our trek. We had left the car in a nearby house of a farmer and a good friend of Paolo. His familiarity with the area and people was rather reassuring then.

What I had seen only in books earlier was now right in front of me – tattooed faces of Kui Kondh women. The women were marvellous, with great pride in tradition and a friendly attitude. I was seeing women with face tattoos for the first time and I really liked it. I took some pictures of them. I loved their colourful saris and the gold studs in their noses.

I am a non-professional photographer and a video maker, but photography has been my first passion since my teens. Photography is a way for me to keep memories of what I experience when I travel and a way to share with my loved ones what they haven't had the opportunity to experience with me. For me there is never a particular reason to take a picture. It's just a way to freeze a moment, a subject, a special attraction, and keep it with you for future enjoyment. As a photographer, I am mainly attracted by faces and the expressions in the eyes. They represent the inner life of the subject.

A fan of close-up photos, I took some pictures of the women, focusing on details such as the earrings or the tattoo itself. We took photos of them with my camera, they took pictures of us and with us on their mobile phones.

I would *never* take a photo if not allowed by the subject itself but how do I convince the commander? He is adamant that we abused the tribals by clicking their pictures.

Despite the obvious poverty of their condition, the tribals had serene expressions and they were happy to be photographed, as if eager to share their tribal origins. With pleasure we accepted their invitation for a drink and got talking.

What surprised me was that many family houses were so isolated from each other, instead of being set close to each other to establish a sort of little village. Maybe this was how they preferred to live but wouldn't it be convenient to be closer together? Even for the government it would be easier to deliver the basic facilities that I am yet to see in these villages. Imagine constructing kilometres of road to lead to just one house. That may be a little impractical and perhaps this sparse and isolated habitation was one reason behind them being left out of India's development story.

Though the poverty was abject I realized that everybody had a mobile phone, even if the signal was very inconsistent. This was a means of staying in touch with each other in an otherwise isolated existence.

Paolo was handing over copies of photos taken on a previous trip. They thanked him for the gift and asked us to take some more photos with them. Then they again clicked pictures with their mobile phones. After these pleasantries we took leave of our friends. I regretted not knowing the local language and therefore being unable to participate in these cheerful chats.

It was hot and sultry when we set out on our hike but I was happy that my much-anticipated plan was finally materializing; the draining heat was compensated for by this convenient arrangement of having Paolo – an Italian interested in tribal life – as a guide. I was grateful that despite the new law against tourism in tribal areas, we could still interact with the tribes without violating the law. But holy law! Here we are told that we have indeed violated the Naxal law! I wish Paolo knew better, but why blame him. These people are blinded by a false notion of power.

It was getting dark so, after a few kilometres of trekking, we decided to stop and set up our tents for the night in a field where the paddy had just been harvested. The cook started preparing dinner: rice, beans and dal. We had our dinner and as soon as it got dark, we crawled inside our tents, quite tired after a long day's travelling. We were up early, at sunrise. A quick breakfast and we hit the trail once more. During our march we crossed farmers at work in their fields who never lacked a smile and a nod. At one point we stopped by a little hut where a family was boiling a huge quantity of ginger roots to be sold at the market. They invited us for a drink and we were happy to be made so welcome. The exchange of chats and smiles went on at least for an hour, with me taking photos of them with my professional camera and them taking photos of us with their mobile phones. It seemed they were as interested in our western style of living as much as we were of their tribal life. What kind people live in this region, always ready to welcome a stranger. But we had to leave; we had to walk for several kilometres before the night set in. In the evening we came to a little hamlet where the inhabitants started cheering us from far away. They were Paolo's friends.

Outside one house, in the dirt backyard, a young man, maybe twenty years old, lay on a typical Indian bed made of rope. His name was Salman and, according to Paolo, in the last three years, he had progressively lost the ability to walk and then to stand on his own feet. Salman had a very open expression. His dark eyes watched us intently, on the lookout for opportunities to have someone new to talk to.

Photo distribution from previous trips took place here too. It seems pictures form a strong sense of memory and friendship. It is also a way of connecting the threads and provides continuity to the conversation from a time that otherwise feels remote.

Once more I felt a bit excluded as the locals at most speak Odia or the local dialect unknown even to Paolo. We found out that Salman had innovated a kind of signal booster for his mobile phone to make it work even in this very remote area. He was an amazing young man with a vivid mind. This boy should be given a better chance in life, I said to myself. Once out of the forest, I would at least send Salman, through Paolo, some books to read.

For the night, we set up our tents in the little church next to Salman's house as the cook started preparing dinner. Before dinner I decided to go to the river to freshen up and get rid of all the sweat of the very hot day. We shared our dinner with Salman and his parents and after some more conversation with our hosts, we went to bed – the perfect start to the kind of journey I had in mind, getting to know a little about the indigenous people and actually getting to stay with them. This is why I had travelled so far – to be with them and see them up close, much like my favourite close-up photographs.

•

At the end of the day I feel sweaty, dirty but there is no opportunity to wash. I wonder if there's a river nearby. The two Indians – the cook and the porter – seem okay with the heat and even Paolo doesn't seem to be particularly in any misery. Probably, after twenty years living in India, he is acclimatized to these conditions. But I am not.

Our cook, who speaks some English, seems to be very concerned about what is going on. He tells me he is the only one working in his family and next week his father has to go through a surgery. He is in tears as he talks about that. The other Indian fellow cannot communicate with me as he only speaks Odia.

This looks to me like a war between the poor that leaves no winners. The Naxalites say they fight for the tribals but by doing that they are hurting a poor Indian guy. All these movements and revolutions are full of contradictions.

And this is above what they are doing to me. Did I say – to me only? I realize I have never really considered Paolo's feelings, his fears, his problems. He has an eighty-five-year-old father, a cardiac patient whose heart may not be able to handle this situation. Paolo's sister had a brain stroke two months ago and she is now in a hospital for rehabilitation. I think I should be less selfish and consider everyone else's feelings in the situation. Last but not the least, I should better appreciate Paolo's request to the commander to free us and keep him as hostage. Though I realize all this, under the circumstances it seems like my own life is the most precious.

When it's time to go to sleep, the commander says that if we like, we can set up our tents for the night but we will have to pack them up in the early morning. That sounds good. Once more the commander shows a caring approach. He and his soldiers sleep in the open air on the ground, just covered by the plastic tarp. I understand they have to be ready to move at any moment, in case the police get wind of them.

Another night in captivity – allowed to sleep inside our tents but with no water for a quick wash. I am lucky I have my wet wipes with which I clean up my body of the salt of the heavy sweat of the day.

16 March 2012

It's my thirty-eighth wedding anniversary. What a day to wake up as a hostage! What must Silvana be thinking; I couldn't even call and wish her. I can only hope they don't get to know of my situation. I still feel we will be freed soon. By now Silvana must have received a big bouquet of flowers and a ring I arranged before my trip to be delivered to her on the anniversary. India is where we came after our honeymoon, India is a place we feel we are in love with and now India is where I may … I can't bear to think that we may be killed. I am sure that will not happen. But it happens all the time around the world. Terrorists or whoever they are torture hostages and kill them if the government doesn't meet their demands.

Early in the morning, after a quick breakfast with tea and biscuits from our food reserve, the group is on the move again. The cadres are overloaded with their firearms, ammunition pouches, little backpacks, food reserves carried on the head in a sack, the pots and jerry cans of drinking water in their hands and, last but not the least, my backpack that I keep refusing to carry. It's amazing how much weight they can carry along these steep trails, dressed in uniforms that seem to me quite heavy in this unbearable humid heat. And their shoes are very cheap canvas sneakers while I am wearing professional waterproof trekking boots.

No one complains.

The way they share the workload is interesting. Just before moving, the second in command calls all armed cadres with a whistle, and they arrange themselves quietly in neat rows. All the stuff to be carried is placed in front of the group and, with no one being told what to do, they come forward one at a time and take possession of the part of the baggage they believe they can bear. This way exposes each one to the judgement of others, so that no one can avoid his duty without the knowledge being in the public domain. Girls aren't less willing than men to carry loads.

I am in admiration of their sense of discipline and conviction to their cause – which of course I am unable to understand as any cause really. But they are driven from within to persevere with this mindless journey and the commander is truly in command of his battalion.

Today the trail is very steep as we are moving to a higher altitude. Every fifteen minutes, true to my adopted role of an old, weak man, I ask for a halt and the commander agrees to take a break. Before giving the order to move again, he always asks me if I feel ready to go. He is quite gentle with me, while I try to exploit his sensitivity. But to no avail yet so far as my release goes.

As we trudge along on this arduous walk, the day heat drains our strength entirely. The line gets fragmented along the climb.

The better in shape go faster while the weaker or those with more weight to carry move far more slowly.

I can hardly understand how it is possible to continue with this kind of life for long. I have been with them only a few days but I have realized that there must be a deep motivation to justify such hardship and sacrifices. In a couple of months the temperature will rise even higher and the humidity will become unbearable. I can't imagine today's hike in that heat. And what happens during the rainy season when there is mud and rain, and moisture is trapped in your clothes twenty-four hours a day? Why do they risk their young lives every day in an endless fight against an overwhelming enemy? I have to talk to the commander about that. I want to understand.

In any case, they are sort of heroes to me, regardless of whether I agree with them or not. What a dream they must have in their mind for them to make such huge sacrifices. And this sacrifice and commitment must be helping them garner local support and recruit more cadres.

After the day's very demanding march, we end up at the top of a hill just an hour before sunset. The girls, without any prompting, start collecting logs for a fire, while the men define the camp limits and set the defence line.

I feel pretty tired. It has been a very long march, but sharing each other's fatigue, the ordeal becomes bearable. The soldiers are also easing up; they are not as taut-faced as they used to be. Sometime I detect a smile. Maybe we feel less of a threat to them.

Once again I ask the commander for a bath. I feel really dirty. I would like to wash out the last two days of grime and sweat. But it will only be possible after sunset. Very likely, all the streams are carefully watched by the Indian government forces, so only after sunset will we be able to go to a local stream for a bath. We set up our tents for the night. I have my own tent, while Paolo shares his with our two Indian teammates. When it gets dark, two armed soldiers, Paolo and I head to a stream. We are requested to avoid using our headlamps as much as possible. It's unbelievable how, in such thick darkness, these people can walk without problems. At every step, almost in the total darkness, I risk an ankle sprain, while the soldiers walk briskly along the dark path downhill; Paolo looks more used to this darkness than me.

Finally, we near a little house in the middle of nowhere. It looks uninhabited, with no lights or noises coming from it, but the bleating of goats by the fence suggests that someone is living here. These people probably do not want to be involved with the turf war in any way. We reach a small stream just next to the house and, after two full days of walking, I finally get a refreshing bath.

It's incredible how just being able to wash in a fresh stream after days of anxiety can make one feel human again. It washes away all worries even if temporarily. The darkness of the night, the smell of soap, the water flowing over the skin, the stars smiling in the sky transport me for a moment from our painful hostage situation. This is the reason why I came here – to enjoy the place in a friendly way. And though I ended up in very different circumstances, yet I am momentarily happy. There is something about water that makes one feel clean and refreshed in mind and spirit. That is why they say water is life.

Having a bath in a stream in the darkness, at the point of a gun, is not everyday life. But I don't want this condition to bias my mind. I resolve once again to try to understand why they are doing this and to what end. Maybe they have a point of view I can appreciate. They are not demanding money from us as abductors usually do. So, what is it they want really?

We head back towards the night camp, where a frugal dinner is waiting for us. After the meal, there is nothing one can do but try to sleep.

17 March 2012

The light of the day wakes us up after a revitalizing sleep. Female cadres are already at work preparing breakfast while a patrol has scouted the neighbourhood to make sure that there are no imminent threats. Before we move, the commander informs us that the two Indians will be released today, carrying a message for negotiation for Paolo's freedom and mine. They will be led to a main road where they will catch a means of transport to Bhubaneswar.

To some extent, this is what I expected. The two Indians are two more mouths to be fed, with low value for the local authorities, while two foreigners are of much greater value in a negotiation. Paolo's concern is that the two attendants can easily be taken as accomplices of the Maoists, so he writes a brief message and delivers it to the cook, telling him to give it to the police once he reaches Bhubaneswar. I'm very happy that the situation is moving but what happens if the local government refuses to negotiate? I express my concerns to Paolo but he tells me that this kind of negotiation in India is quick and dirty. By now the international media must have taken note and the Indian government would do whatever possible to avoid any further embarrassment. This is the heart of India and while they don't mind various levels of insurgency in the far-off areas, here they want to show they are in control.

Paolo tries to convince me that as we haven't done anything really wrong to the Maoists, we should not be afraid.

I think Paolo is trying to keep me calm. You never know in advance how a negotiation will evolve. Negotiations in such circumstances can go awry and infuriate the militia; and they are used to having their guns talk since they themselves won't talk.

In a matter of some minutes everybody is ready to move. Some of the girls sweep away the traces of our presence with branches. I like it; it reminds me of the wild west movies of my adolescence. It's funny how nice feelings mix up with bad ones in these situations. We are slaves of habit and it takes just a few days to get used to a kind of life otherwise unimaginable.

We head in one direction while our cook and the porter go in the opposite direction along with two soldiers. We barely have time to tell them to convey to everybody that we are well and we soon lose sight of them.

Another long day of walking up and down the hills, crossing rivers, climbing mountains, fleeing possible pursuers. We follow a path that seems to be erratic but I am sure it's done on purpose to avoid leaving any clues for anyone following. Once in a while we stop by a bush waiting for a patrol to return, then we head in the opposite direction. We proceed in a single line with a vanguard and a rearguard we can't see. I'm sure the rear is responsible for erasing any traces of our passage. They really know what to do and are very diligent about it. If they want to stay alive, they have to do their best to avoid leaving any traces for pursuers.

And then night comes. We head to a new location for camping. Paolo and I are allowed, once more, to set up our tents. A soldier devotes himself to preparing the site for the night, removing the stones; someone else goes ahead to set up the guard posts; some of the girls head for the nearest water body for water while the one delegated to cook sets up the 'kitchen'. Today I didn't get a chance to speak with the commander. The march has been at a very good pace with limited stops, and during the halts we were asked to maintain silence. They seem to fear we are being followed by the police but their vanguard and the rearguard haven't reported danger.

Today we again ask for the opportunity to bathe at the river and the commander, without any hesitation, gives us permission. He is behaving in a very courteous way with us. So far he has not denied anything to us, apart from our freedom.

The supplies we had with us for trekking are coming to an end. From tomorrow onwards we will have to eat their food. Another night arrives without any news and after a very meagre dinner we go to sleep.

18 March 2012

As usual, at the first light of day, everybody is up doing his or her duty and we too wake up early, packing our tent and getting ready to move. While having breakfast Paolo and I discuss the possible demands the Maoists will make in exchange for our freedom. Paolo tells me that normally everything is resolved with an exchange of prisoners, with negotiations being relatively brief. I don't know the local situation but I won't foster useless illusions. I'm very hands-on and I'd rather deal with problems as they appear.

I think I will ask the commander a specific question.

Very calm and with no fear I go to where the commander is sitting and there ensues a long discussion between the commander and me.

CC: What if the police don't comply with your requirements? Are you going to kill us?

C [with a very peaceful expression]: I have never killed anybody.

How can this be the truth? Are the bullets in their weapons candies? Are they playing virtual war games? But the calm expression on his face and the tone of his voice tells me that perhaps he is speaking the truth.

CC: I don't believe it. If they don't agree with your requests, you will probably kill us.

C: We are not like the police. They come to our places, they arrest our relatives for no reason, they beat them to death, they rape our women and we cannot react if we do not want to suffer the same fate.

CC: And to fight this you kill people and abduct foreigners? From my point of view this is an impossible way to resolve the matter. Look at you – you are more or less twenty people fighting against an army of thousands. The only possible end is the massacre of your small group, no matter how long it will take. The disparity of forces in place is too obvious. And once you are dead, after a few years nobody will remember the reason behind it.'

C: You know, each one here in my group has had a sister raped, a father beaten, a brother deported, a relative killed by the police. We don't see any escape from this fight.

CC: I understand, but wouldn't it be better to fight the system from the inside? Maybe become an activist, a politician, bring to the attention of more people to what is now unknown or misreported in the media and by the authorities. If you do something for the good of the people but it is misrepresented in the media, what you achieve may be the opposite of your intent. If you die fighting, nobody will speak on your behalf. Maybe other Maoists will try to tell the story but the political system will distort their declarations and prevent the message from reaching out.

If you are inside the castle it's much easier to open the castle gate than from outside. Get into the arena, become a politician, fight the system from the inside. If you all participate in the political life, your voice will never be silenced. If you fight with arms, sooner or later they will kill you – and I have never heard a dead man expressing his opinion.

C: [very calmly, after listening very carefully] Until a few years ago I was a politician. I tried from the inside but once I realized it was a hopeless exercise, I opted for armed struggle.

That's really news! He was a politician? I always thought his English was too good for him to be a peasant or a simple tribal. And his way of reasoning is too educated for a simple insurgent. Here I am sitting in the middle of nowhere with someone who was an active politician and from a political family as well and he gave up all that to live in malaria-infested jungles on the run from government forces, trying to give the oppressed tribals a voice. It sounds utopian but he is at least putting in physical effort that he could have easily avoided.

All around us the preparations for departure is hectic, and now the commander is also preparing to move.

CC: Before we move let me say one last thing. Since at any time we can become targets of the local police and the situation is much more dangerous than yesterday, I must tell you that when your men seized us, they forgot to take my mobile phone. I think they didn't recognize it as a mobile. I hope you won't think I have kept it hidden or it has been used against you.'

C: [with no change in his expression – there is neither concern nor anger] 'Don't worry. You can keep it. There are no towers in the vicinity, you won't receive any signal.

And we start off again.

During the day while trekking I continue to behave like a weak old man frequently asking for halts. I think some of the girls overloaded with supplies may be grateful to me for the opportunity to rest every now and then.

A couple of hours before dark we reach a new site, relatively high in altitude. It has been a long walk in a very hot day but at this altitude the air is dryer and relatively fresher.

As soon as we get there, the majority of the soldiers disappear downhill carrying empty water containers on their heads. Two of the girls deploy a big plastic tarp in a wide depression in the ground. After a few minutes the soldiers who had disappeared down the slope of the hill begin to come back with the containers full of water. Each one empties his vessel into the hole protected by plastic sheeting, and heads back towards the source of water. They seem to be creating a water reservoir. Perhaps they fear an attack or are storing water in case they cannot reach the water source later. They are really smart.

The kitchen is set up and the dinner prepared, while Paolo and myself set up the tent for the night and go to the river for a bath, as always followed by two armed people.

Since we have exhausted our own food supply, they offer us the same food everybody else is eating – steamed rice with dal. We attempt to eat it but both Paolo and I are unable to swallow the food. The taste of the boiled rice is terrible. The soldiers eat a huge quantity of it. It is virtually the only food they have every day. We return the plates to the cook, almost untouched, generating a concerned expression on the commander's face. We eat some cookies that were left from our supplies, sitting beside our tents.

Paolo can hear some noise at a distance; he says there is a settlement close by. It seems strange to me that just the day after they made our hostage situation known to the world, they decide to camp near a village. Perhaps they believe they have more support from the local people in this area or maybe consider this as a more defensible location.

But these questions are not going to be answered tonight. We go to sleep tired and hungry.

PART III

Elena

Elena Frova is a manager with Fox TV in Rome. Her boyfriend Daniele is Claudio's son. He was a video animator with Fox at time of Claudio's kidnapping. Daniele and Elena used to live in Grottaferrata, about ten minutes by car from Claudio's house in Rocca di Papa near Rome. Silvana, Claudio's wife, is a homemaker. Valeria, Claudio's daughter, is a psychologist married to Simon Mastrangelo who is an ergonomist.

It's Friday, Daniele and I leave office and head to a nice agritourism resort in the vicinity of Capalbio, in Tuscany, to spend two romantic days. We look forward to enjoying the local food and the peace, and exploring the territory. Lisa, my daughter, is in Germany with her school for the week, and Daniele and I will be on our own for ten days.

And with us is Artù, my little poodle! Daniele is in such a good mood that he has been tolerating the dog to the point that when I give him the leash, off-guard, he takes it for a walk!

We reach Poggi Etruschi quite late but a good dinner is waiting for us, together with the only other guests of the hotel, a Sicilian guy with his Dutch partner.

We talk about everything, from the diversity of cultures to life's pleasures, from kids to vacations, from religion to food.

A little high from the wine and tired, we go to bed and fall asleep holding each other.

Next morning, we take our time to get out of bed. I take the dog for a walk and notice a strange wind outside, almost threatening, but after breakfast we really want to go out to see a property we saw in an advertisement on the Internet.

Renato, the pensione owner, welcomes us with a smile and brings us the greetings of the Sicilian-Dutch couple of the night before who have already left.

We take the car for our tour, dreaming of what we may do if we buy a property in such countryside. What kind of activity we could set up, how much space we will need, whether to grow olive trees or fruit trees, should it overlook the sea or the countryside? Or, who knows, we may look for a smaller property only for ourselves, maybe to make olive oil and spend the weekends escaping from the city chaos. Daniele is addicted – to land, hard work, sweat, nature, the smell of green. Daniele is the sort of person who cannot sit still at a desk. He got himself fired from a permanent contract because he couldn't sit in the office every day. Sitting in front of a monitor suffocates him, oppresses him, yet he is a hard worker, and puts his heart and soul into what he does. But he needs his drug – he needs to feel the smell of the earth, have real contact with people.

I know he sometimes thinks of renting out his house, and living on a few hundred Euros per month, and travelling the world! Since he has met me, he has decided to quit these dreams, but he suffers and perhaps he also needs to invest in something solid for the future. Claudio always says, 'You have to reach a goal that gives you certainty, only then can you enjoy the fruits of a lifetime.' Daniele knows it and knows that I also think the same.

The solution is a property in the countryside. A place to feel the smell of freedom, a place to take care of, just for himself, to hang a hammock and swing listening to the sounds of the country. A place that would save his life, keep him here and calm down his burning desire to wander the world.

We start to feel a little hungry and decide to stop for lunch at a restaurant in Talamone. At 3 p.m. we get to the property; it's not so bad, but a power pylon just in the middle of it dampens our enthusiasm.

It will be really hard to find an area in Pitigliano that has all the requirements we are looking for. We would have taken it up but we must be sure that one can get the licence to become a farmer. Maybe a smaller land would be easier to manage, but in that case, we can't make it a business proposition.

We wander around a little more by car, checking out some small villages in the neighbourhood, and stop for dinner at a restaurant recommended by Simon and Valeria. The restaurant also allows dogs and the waiter brings, without us even asking, a bowl of water for Artù. We eat with pleasure; the palate excited and satisfied, we refrain from drinking too much because we have to drive for almost an hour to return to the pensione.

We leave the restaurant at midnight. We are in the parking lot, ready to jump in the car, when Daniele's phone rings. It's Valeria. 'Two Italian tourists have been abducted in Odisha, an Indian state in the east, and Dad was there.' We hope fervently it wasn't him. Who knows how many Italians are now wandering around Odisha these days? It may be a coincidence, but I feel uncomfortable. Something tells me we should find out more. Okay, let's keep calm, we tell ourselves, but I don't really feel calm. I am going to ask a friend of mine working at the ANSA news agency if he knows anything more.

I can see Daniele looking a bit distraught, even though he is trying to stay calm. He is unusually silent.

Once in the car we talk about it and come to the conclusion that it would really be too strange a coincidence. In fact, there aren't too many Italians trekking in the Odisha jungle, but no, no … it can't be him. These things happen in novels and only to other people, never to us. It is too dramatic.

We get back to the pensione and in bed we hug each other tightly, but we already know that something has changed.

At 6 a.m. the phone rings. It's Valeria.

Yes, it's Claudio. Yes, he is one of the two Italian hostages. The Naxali rebels abducted him, together with Paolo, the local Italian guide with whom Claudio was trekking. They also took the cook and a porter, who were released shortly after, probably because they were Indians.

Oh my God. What can we do? Who are Naxalis?

Daniele just utters a few words and, in the silence of dawn, shuts the phone, turns on his side in a foetal position and grips my hand.

'It's him,' he whispers.

I can hear his deep breathing and the loud silence of his whirring thoughts. His breathing becomes deeper and after some time he falls asleep, curled up. I look at him and my heart skips a beat. I look at him again and I think: his anchor, his role model, his guide, the one who gives him a sense of safety, is in danger right now, very vulnerable and very far away. And if Claudio is vulnerable, Daniele is lost.

I cannot sleep but I don't want to wake up Daniele because I know he will need this extra energy. I get up and take the dog for a walk.

I walk around but I am unable to focus; everything is so surreal, the dew, the cypress trees, the fence with the horses, the strong wind, the forest, the animals, the insects, the trails, the heat, the foreign voices, the marches, the fear of the unknown.

I call my parents. I'm upset, I can hardly speak. I don't know what I'm saying and they are shocked. They say almost nothing, just try to calm me down with a few words. It occurs to me that a few days before, on Facebook, Claudio had written that he was unable to go and see the tribal areas because they were forbidden to tourists and that the long trip he had planned had turned into a five-day trek in the forest. And, just before entering the jungle, he had enthusiastically informed us all that he would call us in another five days. It's been more than five days.

Valeria's caution disguised as a joke on Facebook was obviously of no use: 'I would be starting with a tirade like an anxious mother would do with her teenage son on his first trip … but I avoid it and I hug you. Enjoy your forest!'

But who could ever imagine that something like this could happen to this honest, sincere, sweet lover of humanity, father of two and husband of Silvana?

The year before Daniele went on a similar trip travelling around Kerala, on his own, on a rented motorbike. And when I realized he was in an area where I heard tigers had eaten human beings and runaway elephants had injured villagers, I yelled at him on Skype. I was furious with him because he was risking his life, because he was getting me so worried, because the euphoria of these exotic trips was making him lose all sense of limits, the limits between an escape kind of holiday and an unnecessarily risky holiday.

Then I cooled down because I thought of the statistics. With so many Indians in the area and the many days of the year, with the few tigers around, why should it happen to Daniele? No, I was just overreacting. These things only happen to others, or in the movies.

It's been a while that I have been walking and when I come across Renato, the pensione owner smilingly asks me what I would prefer for breakfast.

I get a knot in my throat, I cannot even answer. It is as if a stone is resting at the base of the tongue and preventing me from moving it. I wave a hand as I approach him, and burst into tears. A human presence, a face, is all one needs to break down and let go. I mumble the news, I tell him that Claudio is Daniele's father and I weep bitter tears.

We quickly pack our luggage, glug down some coffee, check out and leave.

It's Sunday morning and we are heading back to Rome. We want to reach Rocca di Papa as soon as possible and be with Silvana, Valeria and Simon. While travelling we are in contact with Valeria, tired, destroyed; she has spent a completely blank night. Silvana seems to be strong; at least this is what it sounds like when she exchanges a few words with Daniele. But it isn't really so; it is called 'pulling themselves together', but it is not necessarily the same as being strong. How can you be prepared for such an event?

We first go to my apartment in Rome to drop the dog. Luckily, I'm hosting Manon, my close Dutch friend, who will take care of Artù for the next two days. Daniele recovers his car; we buy pizza slices and head to Rocca di Papa. As I drive, I look at the city, I think about its flaws, the chaos, the roads, but now it all seems so nice. I guess Claudio would pay gold to be back in the messy reassuring nest of Rome. I make a few phone calls. I call my boss to tell her I will not be in office tomorrow. I call my sister who, in the following days, becomes my press agent. I again call my parents and sometimes I look in the rearview mirror and I see Daniele following me, driving his car, and the sight of him makes me feel helpless.

Finally, we arrive at Rocca di Papa. Valeria opens the door and I hug her for a few minutes in silence, and then Silvana. I sense her effort to hold back the tears, but her eyes are watery and her smile is just a hint.

Claudio, you have no idea how many people are in the house, I tell myself! Really, a bustle of friends, relatives, neighbours. There are those who make jokes to lighten the tension and those who cannot stop crying, those who ask questions and those who express opinions, those who watch the news on TV and those who navigate the Internet for more news, some call other friends, others smoke in the garden, some answer the phone – it is ringing all the time! – others make tea or bring food. We look like ants, where each one has a specific function; there are the occasional cicadas but most are on the move.

I get a call from Lisa in Germany; I try very hard not to cry and not to show anything in my tone of voice. I listen, I hear her stories, her sweet voice. She doesn't know Claudio has been kidnapped. I'll have to tell her but I don't know when.

Simon is on the phone with the Foreign Office. He is very good at it – calm, polite and firm at the same time. He asks for explanations, he writes down the answers on a pad that he always carries, and that is our regular source of news.

Very little news but we decide on a few things: we must not give interviews, we must not find other channels of information because we could create dangerous overlaps, we have to rely only on the Foreign Office. It wouldn't be wise to depend on newspapers reports. Most of the time, newspapers publish articles with the intent of making news rather than providing real information.

According to the news, Claudio is, among other things, a missionary doctor, an engineer, an employee of a local health authority, a retired man. Claudio is also being called Francesco by some. Others are saying Claudio has malaria and can't stand up and, according to some others, the guerrillas drank water from a river because they ran out of packaged water and Claudio is there for humanitarian purposes. Some said Claudio was kidnapped on Friday, the 16th (it happened on the 14th), that Paolo had been followed for days, that Claudio and Paolo had photographed women bathing in the river. Not one of those news pieces is true.

There are those who wonder what he eats, if he is treated well, how it is to sleep amid insects and strange animals, how long he will be held in custody, how does he wash himself or if he speaks with the guerrillas, was the guide not prudent. We ask ourselves lots of questions and each one gives his own imaginative answers.

The most imaginative of all is Daniele, who imagines his father dialoguing with the guerrillas, trying to know them, understand their reasons, sleeping under the stars with the evocative sounds of the jungle, frightened and worried about upsetting his family but fascinated by where he is, in an out-of-time, out-of-body, surreal experience, profound and unique.

Meanwhile, on the advice of the Foreign Office, Daniele blocks Claudio's credit cards. It's strange to hear him on the phone saying, 'No, I don't have the credit card numbers. I just explained that I'm the son of the Italian kidnapped in India, I don't have the papers with me. Please help me to block them, at least temporarily.'

At home, journalists continue to buzz and Valeria, the bulldozer, rejects them, gentle and firm at the same time. A few photos of us end up in the newspapers: Ilenia (daughter of Rosario, Claudio's cousin) peeking out between the curtains of the salon, Franco and Loriana (Claudio's brother and his wife) entering the house, myself on the phone in the garden.

The mayor comes home; he expresses sympathy and support, and agrees to our request to avoid interviews, or at least not to go into too many details, as required by the Foreign

Office. In spite of this, the day after, he sends a local civil servant proposing to make a huge sign to be hung in the town's main square that says 'Release Claudio' with his photo attached! We smile, thank and reject the offer.

At dinner that Sunday there are still a lot of people at home. The fireplace in the kitchen is always on. We realize that we did nothing but eat all day. Anyone who visited the house brought some food – pasta and chickpeas, spaghetti, ratatouille, pizza, meat, cheese, pastries, ice cream, wine. We need to just keep going.

We speak of the beautiful bouquet of roses on the piano. It has been sent by Claudio to Silvana for their anniversary on 16 March, along with a ring and a note: 'I am not as far away as you might think'.

Claudio has been in the custody of the kidnappers for the last few days, but Silvana, Valeria and Daniele had no idea. Obviously. Silvana tells us she was waiting for a call from Claudio after the fifth day in the jungle, at the end of the trek. He said he would call. But the call didn't come. She waited the next day but still there was nothing. Then she heard the news about two Italians being abducted in Odisha. Her blood froze, she stayed up all night and at dawn she heard that it was indeed Claudio.

Claudio is now incredibly far away …

Claudio

In the morning when we wake up I notice a female soldier has changed from her uniform into plainclothes. She is talking intensely with the commander who gives her what looks like a small piece of paper that she pushes into her bra, then she heads downhill.

I think they're sending a messenger to the village, giving instructions about negotiations. I can't seem to give up hope.

The cook brings us some tea and chapattis. At least we have something to eat.

Each soldier is in position, busy creating a shelter from the sun with branches or placing pieces of cloth. After packing our tents for the day, we look for the best-shaded spot to sit. It's not so easy. The trees are very sparse and the soil is full of ashes from the recent fires. One soldier helps us to clear away stones from a spot and make it relatively comfortable. They are always very kind to us. They usually tend to us before getting on with other chores. I think the commander would have given precise directions about that. Everybody has been very respectful so far and apart from the physical strain of walking and mental anxiety of being held a hostage, it has been an incredible adventure.

For the first day since our abduction we will not move at all.

I keep talking to Paolo, telling him about my family, my dreams, my thoughts, and he tells me about his life story and his choices. He left Italy almost twenty years ago to live here in Odisha, to experience the local culture, to be in contact with the tribes. He has lots of interests. He speaks more than five languages; he is a fine sitar player, a chess master and a karate black belt. I never imagined that such a wealth of qualities and knowledge was hidden behind what appears to be a very simple man. The more he tells me, the more I impressed I am. He is a man capable of excelling in many things, but to maintain a lifestyle consistent with his views, he is willing to give up much of what many of us would consider necessities.

He is concerned that what is going on may ruin his chances of being able to continue his life in India. I try to reassure him. I don't see why he should give up all this if he doesn't want to.

After a couple of hours of talking we are tired of sitting around.

The commander is sitting near us and I ask him if I could disturb him.

C: You don't disturb.

CC: You know, we are not as busy as you all during the day, and this is very boring. Is it possible to have a deck of cards or something like that to make the time go faster?

C: [Nods his head] We will see. We will do our best.

CC: Are we going to stay here for long?

C: I don't know.

CC: Do you have some time to talk? I would like to understand something.

C: Yes, of course.

CC: What's your objective with this kind of war?

C: Our objective is to defend the interests of the ethnic tribes against the state and the multinationals. The territories are given in concession to multinationals for the exploitation of natural resources such as minerals or timber, without taking into consideration that these lands are used by peasants for cultivation, for the survival of their families. No one amongst the local inhabitants gets any benefit out of this exploitation.

An excise policy was adopted by the government way back in 1974 banning commercial vending of intoxicants in tribal areas. We want that to be implemented without any delay. In the name of Green Hunt or other operations against us, the government is grabbing more and more green areas using force. It is like the Gold Rush in United States where it was believed that the only good Indian is a dead Indian.

Even Roosevelt uttered those words. The aim of Green Hunt is to capture the resource-rich tribal belt. I will explain the Fifth Schedule to you some day. Under this Green Hunt, they banned many mass organizations and we are protesting against that. We want to raise the level of administration in Scheduled Areas and we have a thirteen-point demand that is with the government right now. Your release is being negotiated based on those demands.

Damn! I think to myself. My freedom will now depend on such serious land issues?

CC: And to defend these reasonable interests you raise a rifle? To do what you think is a must you involve other people, like your young people, in the very dangerous game of war?

C: No one forces them. Each of them has suffered abuse by the police – either they themselves have been abused or a family member. Maybe a raped sister, a beaten father, perhaps a relative imprisoned without specific charges and without a trial. That's why they became Maoists.

CC: If you experience this kind of injustice, I can understand the temptation to take the law into your own hands, but what are the absolute limits of a civil society? Who decides what is right and what is wrong? Who should be punished and how they should be punished? Are you sure that the people who you say you defend agree with you? Who gave you the mandate to act on their behalf? I don't think that peasants enjoy living between armed factions.

C: We defend the peasants from abuse. We keep watch so that no one makes or sells alcohol, which is the bane of the poor. We fight against the settlements of multinationals exploiting natural resources. We try to resolve local conflicts.

CC: But, are you sure that local people are happy about that? I would like to make my own alcohol and drink as much as I like, so far as I don't hassle somebody else's liberty. Why don't you ban tobacco as well? Tobacco undermines the health of people in the same way as alcohol. I think that the state or whoever is considered a superior entity should leave people to their personal freedom, until that freedom impacts anybody else's freedom.

C: You are a hyper democrat. People need to be educated.

CC: I don't like that statement. Hitler wanted to 'educate' the German society as well, but we know the results. I like the idea of educating people but not with a firearm. It's too easy to get an agreement when you ask for it when pointing a gun. Let's talk with people, let's convince them. Once you convince them by the strength of your ideas they will follow you with no need for firearms. And thousands of people sharing the same idea can do much more than twenty people with a few guns.

C: You don't know the reality of India. It's very hard to move an elephant without threatening it.

CC: Gandhi fought the British empire by the force of his convictions, involving millions of people in his dream without resorting to killing.

C: I do not like Gandhi, he was a Brahmin-caste supporter.

CC: I don't agree with you. Gandhi fought a bloodless revolution. He could not expect to win against the British empire and at the same time fight the local leading castes. In due time, once an independent nation was created, the caste system collapsed under the pressure of the people.

And this exchange of ideas goes on for a couple of hours without either party giving way. Half the day is already gone when the commander excuses himself from the conversation to draft the official declaration that will be delivered to the negotiators to be broadcast nationwide.

Time slows down when you are in captivity with no specific duties to do. At lunchtime, we see the girl assigned kitchen duties bringing us mashed potatoes, chapattis and tomatoes. Wow! What luxury, I love mashed potatoes. From now onwards, I say, mashed potatoes forever – much better than the unbearable boiled rice of last night. It's great to have something to eat that we both like.

'Would it be possible to get some fruit, maybe tomorrow?'

'We will see,' says the cook.

The afternoon gets very hot and tedious, and we slowly move around trying to find spots where there is some shade. At the night, we go for our now standard bath in the river downhill, and after a modest dinner of mashed potatoes, chapatti and tomatoes we retire to our tents.

At dawn, we awake to noises from the field, though the activities are less intense than the previous days' as we are not supposed to move now.

Near the kitchen spot I see a couple of chickens with their legs tied. That's good! Maybe we'll have meat soon. It's been more than a fortnight that I have had a non-vegetarian meal. My trousers are getting loose on me. I must have lost quite a bit of weight from the combination of the forced diet, the extensive walking up and down slopes, and the heat.

We have our daily tea and chapattis at breakfast, then we are called by one of the soldiers holding a radio. There is an English news broadcast.

We now hear that the Maoists have posed a series of requests for our release.

It is the first time ever that my name is in a national broadcast, and what a reason to be part of it!

> The Maoists in Odisha who have abducted two Italian nationals – Claudio Colangelo and Paolo Bosusco – on the 14th of March have finally made their thirteen-point charter of demands public. Drafted on the 16th of March, the release has demanded among other things an immediate halt to all combing operations, strict laws prohibiting tourism in tribal areas, release of all prisoners allegedly implicated in false Maoist cases including Subhashree, wife of top Odisha Maoist Sabyasachi, as well as leaders of people's movements across the state, lifting of the ban imposed on the CPI (Maoist)

> party and several frontal organizations, severe punishment for all police personnel involved in custodial death cases and rape, immediate stop to all forms of repression in Posco and Vedanta project areas and free access to drinking water, medical care, irrigation and education up to the high school level in all villages in the state.[1]

Okay, so his wife is also a Maoist and our release is being bartered with that of his wife? That is rather selfish of him, and contrary to his revolutionary posturing.

The Maoist release has called upon the people to agitate and force the state government to concede to their demands. However, it does not mention any deadline nor name the interlocutors who could possibly represent them in any form of negotiations with the state government.

It appears to me that in a democratic and free country it should not be necessary to abduct tourists to achieve those goals. It's not up to me to judge whether police officials have or have not done what is claimed but a proper investigation wouldn't hurt the civil coexistence of these populations. Though the broadcast did mention, I wanted to double check and speaking with the commander, I was now sure that one of the rearrested persons after being acquitted in different cases happens to be his wife.

These men and women are fighting, endangering their lives and those of their loved ones, to pursue an ideal, to give to their children, when born, a future with greater certainty.

Undoubtedly, the bloody revolutions that have occurred in the North African countries have shown that political situations unsustainable for many years, but behind those revolutions there were whole nations convinced of the need for a change. Here we are in the presence of a few who, unasked, claim to represent the majority. In this way, I fear that a creeping dictatorship of the few may substitute what, to their eyes, is deemed to be an imperfect democracy.

I abandon these political considerations and approach the girl cooking for the day. To my surprise I spot plenty of apples and eggplants. Wow, one of my favourite vegetables! I will show them how to cook eggplants Italian style: fried.

Today we have mashed potatoes, chapatti, fried eggplants and apples. A gourmet meal in the middle of the jungle!

Later, after lunch, the girl who went out as a messenger comes back to the camp.

I immediately take a newspaper from her to read about the negotiation developments, but instead of negotiations news, I find something more interesting: details of local political quarrels related to our abduction and the state government's statements against the opposition's attack. How miserable these politicians are! Here we are facing an uncertain future, not sure of our own lives, and there they are squabbling amongst themselves.

One newspaper article speculates that the central government may have sent Paolo and me to track the Maoists and embarrass the local government. How ridiculous is this – to tag us as Indian agents trying to snoop on the Maoists posing as tourists.

Paolo and I are being treated as puppets in the hands of politicians. They are ready to exploit anything for political purposes. They do not care that lives are at risk, families in difficulty or people are defending ideals; the only purpose of their activity is their political interest.

In a while I give up reading the news.

The commander comes to us and drops a deck of cards, a chessboard with chess pieces, newspapers and a couple of propaganda leaflets written in English. Ah! We now have something to kill the boredom. For days we have been just whiling away our time hoping against hope and putting up with the incessant heat of the jungles of Kandhamal. I can see that some fruits and butter and bread have also come from the market.

I ask Paolo if he wants to play cards and he says yes. Soon I realize that I am not able to focus. I just cannot concentrate. I was hoping a game or two would help me de-stress but it obviously hasn't worked. I then suggest chess, making it clear that I'm just a beginner, unlike him. Therefore, I am given some basic training. For about an hour he recounts strategic explanations of tactics in chess. Chess is a rather feudal game with the king having a chance to save himself while the pawns have no right to retreat; they either move ahead or get killed. On the contrary, this is also democratic because the pawn has a chance to become the king! Paolo is a master of the game. The battle begins and in no time, I find myself beaten without having figured how. Cards failed to interest me and now chess makes me feel like a loser.

Looking around, about 10 metres from where we are, I see a group of male and female soldiers sitting in a circle while a girl is reading aloud the news from the local newspaper. I suppose that most of them do not know how to read and this way allows everyone to be updated. The reading is followed by a lively discussion where everyone expresses his or her opinion. I am sorry I cannot understand their language; I'd love to have this opportunity to participate in their discussions. I think it would be enriching for me and everybody else. Discussing only among themselves prevents them from appreciating opinions that are not aligned to the Marxist ideology. The reading and the discussions go on for more than one hour.

I also observe another very important aspect. The general atmosphere has slowly changed. Faces are more relaxed and firearms are leaning against the trees all around the people seated in circle. I think that everybody has finally realized that Paolo and I are not a threat to them in any way. Our quiet and relaxed attitude must have convinced them that we will not do anything that might create problems.

The time seems endless. Sometime in the afternoon the commander comes to us and says, 'We are going to move. Claudio, tomorrow you are going to be released.'

My heart leaps in my chest, tears rise to my eyes and my throat tightens up, but true to my way of being I say, 'I don't believe it, I don't believe it until I am truly free.'

To avoid being hurt, in my life I always avoided excitement or happiness about promises or things that have to be verified, or extreme highs and lows. Perhaps for the same reason I was not particularly frightened at the time of capture, nor do I have any particular anxieties about my future during these days. I prefer things to happen before I manifest my feelings. But, nevertheless, I regard this as a positive sign.

The camp is dismantled, every sign of our passage obliterated and in single file we begin this next journey into the unknown, at least for Paolo and me.

After three hours of trekking downhill, we stop on the other side of the stream, in what can be described as an open field. Only a few stalks of bamboo are left, the rest is ashes. A patrol continues downstream to verify that there are no imminent threats. After one hour the patrol gets back. We are going to camp here tonight.

Today is a new day, maybe the day of my release, but I should not count on it too much, I tell myself. We have breakfast but

I don't see any sign of further movement. Very soon the day becomes hot. The few clumps of bamboo that have withstood the fire provide a shy shade from direct sunlight. With the hours passing, the air becomes unbearable. I think it must be at least 40 degrees and the humidity is soaring. Paolo and I try to make ourselves a shelter by hanging a tent curtain on some bamboos. But after a couple of hours the sun turns in the sky and where there was shadow there is full sunshine. Even the soldiers lie motionless under makeshift shelters, trying to protect themselves from the sun.

The commander, close to our 'shelter', seems indifferent to the heat as he sits under a cloth stretched above him to give him a little shade. He keeps writing on a notepad. The day moves slowly, too slowly today. Maybe it's yesterday's promise of release, maybe it's the heat, maybe it's the motionlessness existence, but the day seems endless. It is lunchtime. No changes. The infinite afternoon depletes my last energies.

The patrols have gone ahead and have even come back. In the late afternoon, when the sun disappears behind the hill, the commander tells us we can go to the river to bathe. I have never craved a cool water bath so much as today. I have been in the Amazon forest once where the humidity was terrible, but today the heat is unbearable.

We take a long and refreshing bath, and we don't want to come out of the water. After almost half an hour other soldiers come to the river to bathe and say that in an hour we have to be ready to move. There will be a quick dinner and then a long walk.

And the walk starts. The soldiers' faces look relaxed and almost happy. It may be a good signal. The trekking pace is quite speedy. There isn't the usual silence of the other walks; the soldiers talk to each other in more than whispers. The line stretches and shortens according to how difficult the path is. As soon as it gets dark we are allowed to use our headlamps as long as we screen the light with the hands. The walk goes on for very long. I estimate we may have walked for more than 15 or 20 kilometres, mainly along a river. The path is sometimes quite difficult and my headlamp is welcomed even by the soldiers who normally walk in the night like cats.

Tonight I am not behaving like an old, weak man. There are many soldiers left behind me.

I think we passed by a village but I cannot say for sure. I heard some noise on the other side of the river. We now encounter a village house and the commander exchanges some words with the house owner. It seems there is no concern about the police knowing about our presence.

At certain moments the line stretches so much that I feel almost alone. No one is in front of me or behind me for maybe 50 metres, but in the dark it is hard to tell. But I cannot afford to hide or run away. I don't know where I am and, last but not the least, soon, if not tonight, I could be released. I need to hold on for some more time. At least nobody is hurting me physically.

I distract myself by thinking of the people around me. In the last few days I have been able to appreciate their discipline, order and cleanliness they were trying to maintain despite the impossible logistics. The weights they were able to carry during the walks were truly remarkable.

Strangely, their attitude towards me has always been detached, maybe because we cannot communicate. I remember once when Paolo and I were in the river in the evening to wash, the guard sent to keep watch on us said to Paolo in Odiya: 'Do not be afraid, we never kill people like you.' The soldiers look fierce but I think most of them feel sorry for us. I am always envious of Paolo because he is able to talk with everybody and, after a while they become friendly with him. I am only able to talk with the commander!

Deep in the night we pass through an area where stumps of trees are still burning from a fire. A lot of smoke, heat and ashes can be felt, increasing the temperature.

Finally, we stop in a bush and settle for the night.

You see, even today I will not be released, I say to myself. I don't want to ask the commander about it, because I don't want to give him satisfaction of his hostage begging for mercy. Maybe it is their sadistic way of torturing us slowly.

In the morning, we are woken up very early to undertake another long walk, up to lunchtime. The female soldiers look really exhausted, overloaded with their belongings, machine guns and supplies. For the first time, I feel compassionate and I take some of the load from one of them.

The guerrilla tactic is to keep moving to be at an advantage over your enemy. But in this heat and deprivation this appears mindless to me.

When we settle down at camp again, I feel totally depleted. We walked very long and we ate very little in the last two days and yesterday's heat didn't help at all.

The area where we settle is quite rocky and it is not easy to find a flat spot to rest, but there are big trees just next to a little stream and so this spot guarantees sunshade and water to bathe whenever we want.

Everybody around us is excited; I see a lot of smiling faces. Soldiers are relaxed and machine guns are left unattended all over. Two guard positions are arranged on the sides of the camp, in the highest area. The girl in charge of the kitchen hurriedly starts putting together a fire to cook. I think everybody is really hungry. We have not eaten a proper meal in the last thirty-six hours. The boiled water reserves are almost finished so another fire is set up to boil water to drink. The camp looks like a nest of industrious ants. Paolo chats around with the soldiers and I lie down doing nothing. It's very tedious and frustrating. I think the commander has made it clear to his soldiers that we should be relieved from any possible duty but I would have preferred to be involved in some activity instead of having nothing to do.

At lunch, the commander informs us that tonight I will be released to journalists who have travelled to this camp to report on our abduction. Maybe this time the statement is true, I say to myself. Since it is an announcement about something to be carried out in a few hours I suppose it is reliable. But we will find out very soon where things stand.

The afternoon seems infinitely treacherous. The time has slowed down dramatically. Thousands of thoughts cross my mind. My family awaiting my release in desperation, people watching the news on TV, the Maoists waiting for their counterparts to keep their promises, the soldiers proud to achieve something with their action, myself going back to my daily life, my regrets about my inability to understand the Odiya language, which has prevented me from really appreciating what has gone on around me.

Before dusk, the commander and four soldiers move away from the camp to meet with the negotiators. Yes! This is the time. This is really happening. I am going to be released. But I better keep cool, you never know. Negotiations infamously break down or get delayed. The Maoists will not let go of this opportunity so easily without exacting their pound of flesh.

After two endless hours and a dip in the river, I am told that we are going to be here for the night. Once more expectations are dashed. And once again, I did well avoiding over-enthusiasm. I am not going to hope and dream again. This has been killing me more than the heat and the humidity – this half expectation of freedom.

As the night comes, the big rocks all around us start releasing the heat stored during the day. We have come downhill quite a lot, and at lower altitudes the air is even more humid, increasing the sensation of heat. I lay in the tent with the zip opened to get some airstream. I know it may be dangerous because of the risk of malaria but the heat and the humidity are too high. After a long time, I finally doze off.

At some point, I sense movements outside. I can hear the commander's voice speaking to his soldiers; the cook revives the fire to prepare breakfast, which makes smoke invade my tent. But I refuse to get up. I will not give satisfaction to the man who, once again, broke a promise. I don't like him right now. I don't want to ask anything, I don't want a further promise. Let me wait and see what happens.

The soldiers continue in their daily routines and the atmosphere continues to be relaxed, the faces showing less stress than in earlier days.

After breakfast the commander comes to us and says, 'Claudio, you are going to be released in a couple of hours.'

Perhaps in a few hours I will be able to talk to Silvana and the kids to relieve their anxiety about my condition. I immediately decide to shave. I didn't shave during captivity and I now look like an old man with a grizzled beard. I've never been used to having a long beard. I don't want to come back to the 'real world' as a weak old man.

I feel regenerated from the news. I want to be in my best shape. I want to give my family the best possible impression. I also want to give a positive signal. We have been treated so respectfully and my appearance should be an indicator.

I ask the commander if they have a razor and shave foam. Done. I am ready. The minutes become hours and nothing happens; then, all of a sudden I hear, 'Come on, let's go.'

I look into Paolo's eyes and he does the same to me. Tears well up but we avoid becoming too sentimental. We share a long, strong hug, then I head to the path, turning back one last time to wave at Paolo. I see an expression of deep sadness in his eyes that grips my heart. That look will never erase itself from my mind.

It's only the commander, three soldiers and I along the track heading to the meeting point with the journalists. The soldiers and the commander have their faces shaded by scarves.

One hour of walking and we reach a wide open area among the trees where I see three men waiting and a couple of cadres on the lookout.

One of the men holding a video camera immediately starts shooting, while the other two have big smiles on their faces.

'Welcome back, Claudio, how are you?' they say.

'Thank you, I am pretty well,' is my short answer.

The soldiers strategically monitor the area while the captain sits on a tarp with the two journalists and begins an interview. I suppose that it is one of the things agreed for the release. Maoists need to gain international visibility and an interview by journalists is certainly effective in this regard. Questions are posed to me by the journalists and I give answers with no particular enthusiasm.

The memory of Paolo's face at the time of my departure from the camp is torturing my mind. Why should I be freed and he be kept for longer? We didn't do anything wrong to the Maoists. Isn't that clear enough by now? But I can't do anything about that.

The interview goes on for almost an hour and at the end of it the commander gets up and tells us we can go. Two cadres will escort us to the valley, to the limits of the forest.

Before leaving, I shake his hand and say, 'I cannot say it has been a pleasure to meet, you but I thank you for the way you treated us. Please, take care of Paolo.'

Then I head downstream without looking back. Ten minutes later, the two cadres bid us farewell and disappear in the forest. An open field and a small house appear on the bank of a river.

I am finally free. There are no pronounced sensations in my mind. Almost the same feeling and attitude I had at the moment of abduction. How strange my reactions are. Is something wrong with me? Or is it just numbness?

I look around. The landscape is peaceful and the trees are the same as before, the only real difference is the lack of firearms in the surrounding. Why should firearms ruin this wonderful area? The peasants are at work in their fields and look at us without any particular interest. We get to the house where the owner offers us seats in the shade. The journalists say that this is the house where they slept the previous night. They had to walk for hours the day before to reach the meeting point with the commander and the effort was too much for the older lot. And that was the reason why the release was postponed to today.

Elena

It's evening. Almost everybody has left. Simon has already spoken several times with the Foreign Office and there's very little information. We know that the guerrillas have sent a list of thirteen demands in exchange for the hostages.

The news begins and, for the first time, we see Claudio's picture full screen – the one with the Indiana Jones hat. While the journalist speaks, Silvana bursts into tears. A sharp cry of pain, followed by rhythmic sobs. Daniele hugs her from behind while she covers her face with her hands. I feel Silvana's pain. I am moved and I can't hold back my tears. We look at each other and realize that we are all tuned into the same feeling. The pain of Silvana, Valeria and Daniele enters us and, with them, we live this surreal experience.

Valeria, who has now been awake for more than twenty-four hours, decides to go to bed. The rest of us try to watch the movie *The Intouchables*, but I fall asleep with my chin on the palm of my hand on the kitchen table, Silvana falls asleep on the deck, Simon and Daniele manage to watch it till the end.

Then we all go to bed. Daniele and I are in the room where he used to sleep when he still lived with his parents, Simon and Valeria in Valeria's room and Silvana, alone, in the master bedroom. In our room I find photos of Daniele when he was sixteen. I can't help laughing. He looks very funny – a broad grin, the big ears and a terrible haircut. From those pictures you'd never know that one day he would have looked like a wild Indian, with a beard and long black hair, tribal necklaces, Bermuda shorts, checkered shirts and boots!

It's Monday. I have decided not to go to work. Others too stay back. Another hectic day, with people dropping by. In the morning, Valentina, one of Valeria and Daniele's cousins, Federica, who is Valeria's close friend, Valeria and I decide to go buy some fruit in Grottaferrata. Daniele and Stefano, Valentina's partner, head to the supermarket. It's a way to get out of the house for some fresh air.

We are out for just about one hour and when we get back home, we find the official who has come on behalf of the mayor. Silvana is talking to him and she lets herself go a little, telling him what an honest, good and prudent man Claudio is. She tells us we are in contact with the Foreign Office and something more, but it is already too much for Valeria who, from behind, is signalling to her mother to cut the conversation short. As soon as the official leaves, Valeria yells at Silvana. She scolds her like a child without even allowing her to speak, and ends by saying, 'Don't spend more than three minutes with anyone, just say, "Thank you and goodbye."' Then she turns on her heel and goes into the kitchen.

Silvana smiles, she understands but mutters, 'I didn't say anything compromising. You have to be kind to those who come to offer help.' A few minutes later Valeria apologizes to Silvana; she knows she's absolutely right but maybe she has been a bit rude. Of course, this becomes the motif of the day – all of us imitate Valeria's posture when she shouted at Silvana, and we burst out laughing. A few hours later there will be another scene that will be part of the collection 'Oui, Valeria c'est moi'.

Meanwhile, the TV news continues to show the kidnapped tourists, adding nothing but imaginative interpretations of Claudio's life. Simon continues his training as a future diplomat in the service of the Foreign Office and his communication efforts are organized and rational, pure ergonomics! Towards evening, among other friends of the family, arrives Giampaolo, Daniele's best friend,. whose nickname in the Roman dialect is 'Er marana' (The Ditch). We go out with him to the street, smoking a cigarette, talking, and there is a lovely spring breeze.

Two people approach us asking whether we know where Claudio Colangelo lives. 'The intercoms are at the compound entrance, but then we can't work out which house they live in and we can't find the right one,' they say.

We look regretful and say, 'We have no clue, we are just guests of another tenant and we really don't know anything about this Mr Colangelo.'

The journalists don't know that they just talked to Claudio's son.

They take leave of us and stand in front of our house's intercom – luckily Valeria removed the name yesterday – and then continue up the street. We quickly get inside before the reporters decide to come back.

As soon as the intercom rings, Valeria frowns, flares her nostrils and thins her lips. She is in charge of the intercom and so she goes to answer it.

'Hi, am I talking to Claudio Colangelo's daughter?'

'No, thanks,' she says in the tone of a programmed robot.

'But if you are the daughter, can you tell us something about your father?'

'No, thanks,' she replies.

'Look, just a couple of words? How are you?'

'No, thanks.'

'I am a reporter for the *Messaggero*, please tell me something.'

'No, thanks.'

We begin to perceive the absurdity of the situation and we nod to Valeria to terminate the conversation. Of course, 'no thanks' becomes another constant leitmotif.

After dinner, I reluctantly go back to Rome, with a heavy heart. I feel the need to just be with them and, above all, to be with Daniele. Unfortunately, I have to go, both because I have to meet my friend Manon, who is about to leave for the Netherlands the next day, and because I have to go to work. I sit up late chatting with my friend who shows her affection and solidarity with the typical discretion of the northern soul. She tells me there aren't many rumours abroad about the case; some newspapers or websites wrote on the abduction of two Italians but nothing more. I wonder how many Germans, Swiss, Spaniards, Brits are seized in various parts of the world and we don't know anything about them. Here in Italy, from time to time, some news emerges of other Italians in the hands of kidnappers – Rossella Urru or Maria Sandra Mariani, hostages for many months in Algeria, the six members of a crew in the hands of Somali pirates– but we know little or nothing. And now we know what their families go through; what a sense of frustration and painful expectancy accompanies them every day at such a juncture

Tuesday morning, I get up early, take the dog out then I go to work. I'm gently accosted by my colleagues. They ask questions or show concern for Daniele and his family, offering words of comfort. All comparisons are between Claudio and Daniele – 'The same! It's in their DNA! Like father, like son!' Somebody even claims that they resemble each other a lot physically, while I think that Daniele is identical to Silvana, not his father. I cannot really concentrate at work; as soon as someone comes up to me I feel like crying and I realize how family also helps you feel stronger. Alone, as now in the office, I feel weak and I want to run away from everyone.

The family ... I'm not used to dealing with such a large family – many relatives, many bonds, many names. I think that if something like this had happened to one of my relatives, there would probably have been at the most a dozen people in the house, and only for the first or second day. This doesn't mean we don't love each other; it's just that there isn't this habit of spending a lot of time together, sharing everything.

At Christmas, I usually party with the family a few days before 25 December, then everybody leaves for different destinations to be with their own friends.

Last Christmas, at my parents' house, we were many! There was my aunt Franca and her husband Guido, my sister Luisa with her husband Claudio, and their kids Riccardo and Flavia, and Lisa, my daughter. Daniele joined us for the first time. So many people! Then I spent the 24th and 25th of December with Daniele's family and the whole tribe. These days I realize that the tribe is much, much bigger!

There is no news about the kidnapping; we only know that the Indian government and the rebels are choosing negotiators to start discussions.

I go through some articles on Maoists and some have a reassuring perspective that humanizes the kidnappers, captures different aspects. It's not like we think – it's not like falling into the hands of fundamentalist fanatics who hate foreigners just because they are western. The hostages, for the Maoists, are tools to open a dialogue with the Indian authorities. Of course, the method is not the most democratic, but we feel this is something positive. At least I do think so, and I also now think that the imaginative thoughts Daniele expressed about Claudio talking and discussing things with the Maoists may not be impossible. Perhaps Claudio is talking to them, maybe he doesn't feel so threatened even though captivity is never acceptable. Perhaps it is true that at night Claudio listens to the sounds of the jungle or watches the stars.

I spend the evening with them. We hear that Claudio got malaria and he is hurt and maybe this could be a reason for releasing him soon. We are concerned about his health but happy that malaria may be a tool for his freedom. The Foreign Office doesn't confirm anything, but it seems clear that the prisoners are in good health and that negotiations have started; now we just have to wait.

Around midnight I get home. I fall asleep at about two in the morning. This is just after I received a text message from Daniele: 'I am thinking of what he is thinking when he is alone in the night ...' My love, so worried about his dad, even though a little voice inside him is telling him he's fine and will return soon.

The next morning I go for an offsite strategy meeting and team building with the entire FOX management in a castle just outside Rome. It's Wednesday. I cannot quite follow the sessions, I am distracted, my head is elsewhere. I take advantage of a colleague's computer to go online and look for news about Claudio. I distractedly catch snippets of conversation around me about various issues – the business strategies to be implemented, the 'death' of television, brand extension, ROI, programme placement, Operation Lazarus, how TV channels must be people friendly, also of resources and coordination systems, and content. Usually all this has meaning for me, but not today.

The team-building games make me feel out of place. To see all these managers acting like kids while developing a fashion show on the basis of the adjectives related to the TV of the future embarrasses me a little. I try to cooperate and participate (because office personnel take notes on how we behave at offsites) and I even manage a smile or a joke. While we are there pretending to save the future of television, Claudio is battling insects and heat and the uncertainty of his life.

As we speak of leadership (leadership within the safe bounds of an office), Claudio has to use his leadership skills with his kidnappers. I get a text message from Daniele: 'Just received the furniture and the new couch that I bought a month ago with the advice and financial support of mom and dad. They are beautiful. Today I cried so much here at my house while I was cleaning the new room.'

I tell the colleagues that I will not spend the night in the castle with everybody else. After dinner, before all my colleagues drown themselves in alcohol, karaoke and childish pranks, I will flee and go home to sleep.

In half an hour I am at Daniele's house. I talk with him and we speak about how Silvana has been dealing with the situation. Silvana has character, she is tough. Fragile in some respects, but strong in others. We agree that these days she is the queen of the stage, handles everyone in the house beautifully, answers the many phone calls, keeps the house clean and has something for everyone. For sure, suffering shines through her delicate and youngish face and often crying takes over. But she is the queen, no doubt.

Thursday morning. I am back to the second day of the offsite. I feel good, I smell the flavour of life in the air, it is the first day of spring. Nothing can happen to Claudio now that it's spring; everything grows, or is created, new colours blossom, new smells emanate. The sessions at the meet are incredibly long and I'm restless, looking forward to being back at Rocca di Papa, being with them all, hugging my sweet love, the wild boy.

At 6 p.m., I jump into my car and leave. Once again I look at Rome with new eyes; even the aggressive drivers in the cars make me smile and I keep hearing a positive note in everything. In Rocca di Papa, it has been another long and eventful day. The roses on the piano have bowed their heads, but they carry on still, proud and tenacious. The photo on the piano, Claudio and Silvana, young and smiling, seems to a good omen.

We order pizza. At dinner there is also Daniele's cousin Gianni who came the day before from Spain, where he lives. There is almost a jovial climate, jokes and teasing. In the background, the fireplace is always blazing and the TV on RaiNews.

I come to find out that in the afternoon they made the cabala. Between laughs and a bit of superstition, they identified the numbers that come out with a few key words of Claudio's arrest, forest, abduction and other. Valeria, Gianni and Linda (one of Valeria's best friends) went to play the lottery numbers and argue about whom, among the people at home, is actually involved in the bet.

We go to sleep at Daniele's in Grottaferrata, but before we go to bed, we talk a bit: about how people behave, how some parents express anxiety and others are laidback. We analyse each other's behavior. I feel a bit strange because I am not a proper relative of theirs and yet Claudio's kidnapping hurts and it also hurts to see the suffering of his loved ones. When my friends and colleagues express their solidarity, I instinctively say, 'I have nothing to do with it, I'm just Daniele's girlfriend,' implying I don't deserve your attention, they deserve it, then I find myself talking in the plural: 'We have just heard from the Foreign Affairs office,' 'We don't know anything more than what the papers say,' 'They tell us that Claudio is fine.'

Saturday morning I wake up early and go to the living room, turning on the TV – it's the usual news loop, nothing new on the eastern front. Tomorrow we are invited to dinner at the home of Simon's parents, but I was planning to make a little trip to Umbria with Daniele, to see another possible piece of land to buy, to breathe good air, and I don't want to run back early for the dinner, so I decline the invitation. Daniele and I talk about the trip and we realize we'd better not move away from Rome and the situation, so we agree to go for lunch with Valeria and Simon at a restaurant on the beach, near Rome, where Cristiano and Daniela had their post-wedding party and where my sister celebrated her fortieth birthday a few years ago. Andrea, a funny and ironic friend of Simon's, joins us.

There are so many people at the beach, some with children, some with dogs on the leash, some smoking a cigarette in the sun, some having a drink on the terrace. Unfortunately, they give us an inside table but we eat heartily. Finally, Valeria is able to loosen up a bit, and for a couple of hours everybody relaxes, we talk about everything. When Valentina and Stefano also arrive, we move to a table outside to enjoy a coffee in the open air. There is a good feeling in the air. Valentina looks up and says that Claudio sees our same sky. Yes, something is going to happen. No one around us could have imagined we are friends and family of Claudio, the abducted Italian.

Around 5 p.m. we go home. Daniele and I have already said that we don't want to go to dinner with Simon's parents and so we are thinking about where to dine when, suddenly, we start getting calls about the release of Claudio and Paolo! We turn on the TV and it is all over the news. We start jumping in joy. I think to myself that maybe we should wait for the Foreign Office to confirm, but I cannot resist and let myself go.

We rush to Rocca di Papa where we find Silvana and Valeria in tears. Valeria is weeping so much that she can't even talk.

Simon gently requests everybody to wait for confirmation. Bravo Simon.

The Indian journalist who had published the photo of the artist who made a sand sculpture of Claudio and Paolo's faces on a beach calls up Valeria and says that Claudio is in a van with two journalists and is coming out of the jungle.

The news of the release has triggered a feast of joy and excitement this Saturday night.

We keep cell phones turned on, next to the bed, in the hope that they are going to blare out like trumpets in the middle of the night with confirmation of the release. We fall asleep, exhausted by emotions too strong for us. The phones don't ring. The Foreign Office is yet to confirm the news. It's Sunday and around 10 a.m. the news says that only Paolo has been released, but shortly after they deny this and say it is Claudio. The Foreign Office is still silent.

Thousands of messages start to arrive from friends and relatives. Television channels and Internet sites broadcast an audio with Claudio's first words as a free man, but I find hard to recognize his voice; we aren't really sure it's him.

To de-stress, Silvana and Valeria go shopping to buy a jacket Valeria needs for work the next day. After that they come to see us at Daniele's house. We are glued to the TV. Rosario, Concetta (Claudio's cousins) and their daughters Ilenia and Gaia join us, and we are all tense. Then a call from the Foreign Office asks for Silvana. We all look at each other and without a word, we understand that the nightmare is over – Claudio has been released.

We listen to Silvana's words, all in silence, as we never did during these chaotic days. She is excited but steady and then everybody screams, as though we had won the lottery or found the elixir for immortality! What crazy joy!

Silvana gets a call from the channel Sky TG24 and her first few words of thanks are for the Ministry of Foreign Office, who was in close touch with the family. She expresses her solidarity with Paolo's family, wishing that they too will soon embrace him. And Silvana's words go in a loop in all the news stories, right after the first words Claudio gave to a journalist of the same news report. Together again, united by satellite – Claudio and Silvana.

Soon after, the Foreign Office manages to get Claudio and Silvana to talk to each other by phone. We eavesdrop shamelessly on Silvana's side of the conversation: 'My love, I'll give you lots of kisses and then a lot of slaps,' 'Come back soon, I'm waiting for you, for Jesus' sake!' Daniele and Valeria also manage to say a few words to Claudio, and then the call disconnects. Meanwhile, on the Internet, there are Claudio's videos of his interviews to the Indian media – he has lost weight but he is in excellent shape; it is our Indiana Jones, he smiles, makes jokes.

There is another call from Claudio, and, as he has already mentioned in some news videos, he says he is in high spirits. Sure, it was tough and the first two days he was afraid for himself and for his family, but then he was treated well, there was a dialogue with the kidnappers, weapons were not pointed at them, they ate, slept, walked with them.

Daniele was right: his visualization of Claudio's prison was the closest to reality, and maybe he was not as far away as we all thought.

Claudio

After the journalists drop me off at the police office in Kandhamal district where I am made to sit for some time, we depart for Bhubaneswar in a police vehicle. I sit in the back seat of the car with two heavily armed plainclothesmen on either side. I don't quite like this; I don't want to be involved in an exchange of gunfire.

It is late in the afternoon and we still have a long way to go before we reach the state capital. At the first village we go through I ask the bodyguards if I can recharge my phone SIM so I can contact my wife in Italy. I do it with ₹1500. I want to be sure I have enough credit to talk with the entire world.

As soon as I recharge my phone, hundreds of messages start tumbling in. Friends, relatives, journalists, everybody has been trying to contact me.

Wow! I didn't realize I had so many friends.

But before reading the messages, I call home.

Finally I'll have the time to talk with my wife and children, tell them what I am feeling right now. It is a long, long call.

It's almost 8 p.m. and the Italian consul calls my number to know how far we are from Bhubaneswar. He is waiting for me at a hotel.

The bodyguards say that we may be two or three hours away.

I haven't slept well in the last few days along with walking in the dark in an unfriendly terrain. But I won't think of that now. The heat is overwhelming and I am feeling really tired.

I request them to move me to the front seat so I can sit more comfortably. I hope all this will end soon.

We are proceeding very slowly due to heavy traffic. I again call my wife to keep her updated on where we are.

While speaking to her, my head suddenly bangs against the windscreen from a strong impact at the back of the car. My phone flies from my hand. Have we been ambushed? But this is not even the jungle!

The two bodyguards jump off the car, their guns levelled.

I try to regain communication with my wife to reassure her everything is fine. I suffered a little blow to my head but I'm okay.

I see the bodyguards threatening a truck driver with their guns. The truck must have hit us on the busy road. The poor man is on his knees pleading with them. I wish they would just let him go and carry on. But that won't happen. We will have to wait for another car to come and pick us up as well as for other policemen to take custody of the poor driver.

I'm thirsty, hungry, sleepy. I'm really, really tired. After almost an hour, a couple of police cars join us. We jump into one, the other takes custody of the truck driver. Let's hope he won't get into a lot of trouble because of this.

I lose track of time.

Finally, we reach a gorgeous hotel in Bhubaneswar where the Italian consul receives me with ease, along with three Italian journalists. Very gently they ask me some questions about my experience but it's more like a talk with friends than an interview.

I'm offered something to eat and drink and, after half an hour, I ask to be allowed to go to sleep. It has been a very, very long day. Maybe the longest and toughest day of my life.

The next day, the consul tells me I'll need to be in Bhubaneswar for another day before I go to Delhi to meet the Italian ambassador, after which I will finally be able to fly back home.

I keep receiving calls from friend, journalists and unknown persons. In the morning three police officers come to meet me. I suspect they are from the intelligence. They are friendly and talk to me comfortably. They want to know as much as possible about the Maoists and I try to give exhaustive answers, avoiding things that, in my opinion, may endanger Paolo's life. How many were there, how well armed, where all did we go and whether I saw anything peculiar to report. I tell them of the walks and avoid telling about my discussions with the commander.

The next morning a police jeep with two heavily armed guys takes me to the airport for my flight to Delhi where I arrive in the afternoon. A car from the Italian embassy is waiting for me. I'm taken to the ambassador's residence, a very nice and spacious house with a lovely garden. The ambassador and his wife receive me like old friends, making me feel very welcome and at ease. I'm offered drinks and some snacks while we spend more than an hour talking about my experience, my family and Paolo as well.

At dinner, there's real mozzarella cheese and Parma ham – mm, what joy! But I am not able to eat very much. I think my stomach has shrunk from near starvation during captivity.

The day after, I wake up very early in the morning and start packing. I exchange warm hugs with the ambassador and his wife and leave for the airport in the embassy car.

On board a flight heading home as I have been many times earlier, but this time the feeling is overwhelming. Everything I see and hear now has a new meaning altogether. My fellow passengers wouldn't guess my story.

I fall asleep.

With a thud the aircraft lands in Fiumicino airport. I am home.

Elena

The wait is excruciating. Silvana has been brave and is holding herself together. I can tell that she is just waiting for the moment when she can see Claudio again. We are pacing up and down in a special lounge at the airport where the Foreign Office has made arrangements for us to receive Claudio. Fortunately, the flying time between New Delhi and Rome is not very long but this wait is killing all of us.

We are informed that the flight has landed. A little later the door opens and we scream. Claudio and Silvana run into each other's arms and hug tightly without uttering a word. They are in tears and are kissing each other. She finally mumbles, 'How are you?' and he says, 'Now, in your arms, I feel much better.' He then hugs his children and we keep kissing each other, reassuring ourselves that the nightmare is over. Claudio is indeed back home.

The police officers accompanying Claudio come up and say that the Public Attorney is waiting for him; he wants to talk to Claudio about the abduction. A Carabinieri car takes him to the Public Attorney's office in Rome while we go home and wait for him to join us.

The debriefing, as they would probably call it, is taking far too long but I guess it is a process with which we cannot interfere.

Claudio is finally home. Silvana hugs him at the door and again we all hug and kiss each other. He looks around intently at his house, the garden, the trees and the surroundings, probably trying to wrap his head around the fact that he is really home amongst his dear ones.

Silvana has prepared a special dinner with his favourite food – eggplant and meatloaf. We ambush him with endless questions and he patiently tries to satisfy our curiosity. He reassures us he didn't really suffer much and they were treated in a reasonably good way, given the circumstances.

It is almost midnight and he excuses himself. To be back in his own bed must be such bliss, hugging and sleeping with his beloved wife.

In the morning, as is his habit, he wakes up quite early and goes to the nearby bar for breakfast – cappuccino and a croissant. He encounters a couple of journalists waiting outside the house gate. But Claudio is firm; he won't give any interviews till Paolo's release. He doesn't want to endanger Paolo's life by saying something wrong. They seem a little upset but understand his situation. The photographers keep clicking away.

At the bar, a huge welcome is waiting for him. Claudio has no idea so many people even know him and would be so happy to have him back. They don't let him pay and everyone has questions for him. Claudio has become a hero!

He returns home after a couple of hours. On his way home two more journalists and a photographer chase him, throwing questions at him and taking photos. He gently requests them to respect his privacy. Paolo is still in captivity. He will not speak until Paolo's release.

The day is a procession of friends and relatives coming to welcome him back home. Lots of smiles, hugs and talks. Claudio is a little embarrassed at having put so many people through such anxiety.

At dinner Silvana has invited all her sisters and Claudio's brothers with wives, husbands and kids. We are almost thirty people partying, drinking and singing exuberantly. I can see the relief and happiness shining in their eyes and in my heart I feel the joy of being part of such a marvellous family.

Claudio keeps telling us about his experiences during the abduction, the thoughts, the worries, and how he was never really scared about the situation. Yes, there was anger, more than any other feeling. Anger against the Maoists because of the worry they were causing his family.

The dinner goes on for more than three hours. 'What a pleasure,' Claudio says, 'to taste good Italian food and wine and to enjoy the warmth of my big family!'

Claudio is finally home and we slowly get back to our own lives. For him though, it is a new lease of life.

Paolo's Release

I was back in Daringbari, where Claudio and Paolo were last seen before their abduction. The town was waiting with bated breath for news of the release of the two Italians. There has never been so much excitement over a piece of news in this hardly-known township.

As we trudge back there after our stint in the jungle, Kailash Dandapat and his men and women welcome us like victorious warriors. He jumps with joy and quickly opens a map on his computer to identify the camp's location. He wants validation of his local knowledge; he claims he knew where we were but kept it to himself.

Daringbari returns to its sleep after drinking tiny cups of tea and relishing vadas in *siyali patta* dishes. Soon it will be over, this disruption by aliens with big vehicles fitted with strange objects which open up to the sky on their own and catches fireflies amongst other things. One more Italian has to be released but that seems only a matter of time.

Soon after Claudio's release, I return to Bhubaneswar simply because I can't bear to be in Daringbari for another day. It's not over yet. Paolo's rescue is awaited but this time I am sure I will not be part of it. Let the negotiators and the government battle it out. I have had enough and am out of it.

But in a few days I am back in sleepy Daringbari and between scourging for news stories, I start taking down notes on where the Maoist movement is heading and how much support it has of the people who inhabit the so-called 'Maoist corridor'.

Kandhamal provides a backdrop of abject poverty and perceived Maoist domination. I try to understand why the Maoists operate in a vacuum where the 'state' has no presence and yet do not attempt to achieve anything for the people they claim they are fighting for. That takes me to villages like Sirkabarga where Indian administration has never cared to even visit leave alone administer. But there is nothing 'Maoist' about the village.

During this period we continue to stay at Kailash Dandapat's Jagruti quarters while others find accommodation in a forest bungalow. In Jagruti's cramped room people drop in all day and that interaction is rare in the township. Our stay here is indefinite and the only way to kill the boredom is to engage in local life. From turmeric to *siyali patta*, I chronicle every aspect of Daringbari life.

After breakfast at the local market we usually do some shooting and eventually end up at the forest bungalow for a cricket match on the uneven lawns. I am not quite sure where the bat and ball came from, though! The previous wait when Claudio was in custody was a tense time, this one much more relaxed; we cook chicken and rice and pour double whiskies too. The heat is intense but the community of journalists – tired of waiting for Paolo's news, yet unable to leave the town – find comfort in each other's company. Someone misses his son's birthday and another his anniversary. A few report unwell but we pull through.

This time I have promised to share the news of release if it came to me. With a non-functioning cell phone network, communication with the outside world is virtually cut off unless we drive off to a distance and catch a signal somewhere. It is easy to identify that point; suddenly on the highway a group of men would be huddled over their phones and one knows immediately that it is a network zone.

It is the middle of the night. We have had a few drinks before trying to sleep. There is a tap on the window and we are told in a whisper that Paolo would be released early morning at a location some distance from Daringbari. We have to leave immediately. I had promised to inform everyone this time, but there is no network and they are in the forest bungalow which is a ten-minute drive from our quarters. I am hoping at least one SMS will go across. I am not being able to keep my promise and it makes me feel awful. Our messenger is frantic and says we cannot waste a minute.

Three vehicles race through the night to an unknown destination, but news had fortunately travelled to the rest of the media and they catch up with us. More than two dozen OB vans zoom through villages that may not have ever seen a vehicle before and arrive before dawn on a road that ends in a paddy field. The wait begins as we have no clue which direction to turn. The intelligence officials had assumed we knew while we hoped they had the inside information. So, we followed each other till we both realized that neither group had the correct news.

Since morning the anticipation of the release had dominated all national headlines. My camera crew places me near a clearing leading into the jungle; I would look back and tell the camera in a live broadcast that 'any moment Paolo is expected to come out from the forest'. My colleagues in the studio are excited but as the hours roll by the anticipation is diffused and we become increasingly worried about what may have happened to Paolo. These are tricky negotiations and anything is possible.

What follows is perhaps the most ridiculous live broadcast situation in my career. I hear on the talkback – the earpiece that connects me to the studio in Delhi – that Paolo is addressing a press conference in Bhubaneswar – which my colleague Sampad is attending – while we are waiting for him to emerge from that forest I keep showing to the viewers! Paolo, meanwhile, had been escorted by a wily negotiator and Maoist sympathizer, Dandapani Mohanty, who took the risk of travelling with him by night without informing anyone. He had been released sometime the previous evening.

So that's how the Daringbari stint ended for us – with a whimper! But even as I returned to Kolkata and settled back to my daily life, those forty-eight hours of trekking the forests and some twenty days of uncertainty have stayed with me, one of the most intense assignments I have been on.

PART IV

Kandhamal

Love Dormitories

> *Aamey ethika loka, aamey koutthu aasinu,*
> *Etthi aamara Bada Pennu achhi,*
> *Etaa Kandha raija,*
> *Tumey kana suni naahan Kandha Raja ku Pana Mantri*
> (We belong to this place, we have not migrated from any other place/ Our God Bada Pennu lives here/ This is Kondh kingdom/ Haven't you heard of Kondh King and Pano Minister?)

In the villages of Kandhamal district in Odisha it is not easy to come across someone who will sit down and tell me stories. Most of the villages are deserted by day, with the people working in fields or in the forests. I finally meet a village schoolmaster on the outskirts of Daringbari who is willing to spare some time. Raghunath Kanhar, a Kondh, is the only teacher of this primary school and has given his students a longer recess. According to Kanhar, the Kondhs believe that one fine day they sprung from the water. In the beginning, everything was water. Nirantali and Kapantali emerged to the earth's surface at Saphaganna. After them came the other gods and the first humans were the Kondhs. But how could they live in water, asks Kanhar, as if to test whether I am listening to him or not. Yes, how did they live in water? Since that was not possible, they went to Nirantali and begged for help. Nirantali then created the earth, plants and other creatures.

So here we have the first amongst humans – the Kondhs – inhabiting the earth. But in Odisha, Kondh is a term used for all tribals and sometimes it is derogatorily used; a foolish person will be called a Kondh.

Kandhamal may have been named after Kondhs but they are all over the place and have migrated/settled across many states. There are the Kuttia, Dongria and Desia or Maliah Kondhs but interestingly marriages between the groups are strictly forbidden even though the language is the same; they all speak Kui. The Kui language doesn't have a script though early British administrators and missionaries wrote Kui in the English alphabet or Odia script. The language became popular because of some amazing riddles in their oral tradition called *bekedi* or *bekeni*.

Little policemen, red turbans on their heads, camp in every house. One gets up, when you call.

It is a matchbox!

It ne'er changes its place, yet travels across the horizons.

Eyes.

It goes out with empty stomach but returns with its belly full.

Pot for fetching water.

King's carpets, none can roll up. None can scratch king's pimples.

Road.

Most references to the Kondhs are about the ritual sacrifice, Meriah, in which human beings were sacrificed. Later they took to sacrificing buffaloes, but that being expensive, the ritual is not performed regularly. Even today Kondhs believe if they are allowed to perform human sacrifice their 'lost glory' would be restored. Meriahs believed they have been created to be sacrificed. Usually they were not Kondhs but were sold by Panas who would kidnap people. Sometimes a Kondh family would sell their children because this sacrifice was also considered honourable. Meriahs were sacrificed to the earth goddess Tari Pinnu in the belief that the blood of the deceased would fertilize the earth and the goddess would bless them with an abundant harvest. Meriahs spent their lives idly, with all their wishes being granted. Consecration of the Meriah would take place a fortnight before the sacrifice; his/her hair would be cut for the first time and decorated with flowers. The village would then indulge in debauchery. Following the orgy, the Meriah would be tortured, prolonging the death as long as possible. It was against this practice that the British sent an expedition to Kondh land after missionaries were captured and offered as Meriah sacrifice.

It was in their war against the Kondhs the British used the term 'insurgents' – probably the first time this word was used. In the Ghumsur war of 1837 the British conquered Kondh land. The rising of the Kondhs of Ghumsur, led by Chakara Bissoyi, was primarily against British interference in the traditional custom of human sacrifice but was also intimately related to resistance to British revenue demands. But it was not until the Kondhs uprising of 1878 in the Rampur district of Kalahandi, that rights and control over the produce of the land became the narrative of Adivasi revolt.

Even before this war, in 1757 French General De Bussy had invaded Ghumsur but was defeated. The British tried to capture the area several times to exact taxes that the tribals were supposed to pay to the kings and finally annexed the area accusing the raja of being a rebel. The raja apparently, along with his family, took refuge in the hills with Kondh tribals.

The reason for such a long-drawn war may not have been stiff tribal resistance as much as the deadly cerebral malaria which claimed many British soldiers and officers. Malaria still stalks these hills and valleys.

After Independence in 1947, the Kondhs became part of the political process with the Representation of the Peoples Act, 1950. In 1952, they voted in the first general election. Reportedly it was the 'outsiders' who cast most of the Kondh and Pana votes. Panas are scheduled caste Hindus who have lived with the Kondhs in Kondholand but have been subservient to the Kondhs. According to Dr Krishan Kumar, the collector of Kandhamal in 2008, of the over 650,000 people in the troubled district, at least 53 per cent are tribals, while less than 20 per cent are Christians. Of the nearly 118,000 Christians, a majority has converted from Dalit families.

In the 1950s there was no electricity, no piped water, no sewage system and no telephone. No one read newspapers. They had so little and used even less that they hardly produced garbage! Today, it's a stark world of poverty, disease and exploitation by moneylenders.

Even at that time when Verrier Elwin wrote about the Kondhs, 'they were grossly oppressed by Dom moneylenders and Patro landlords; they had a hard time from the officials of the Forest Department; their simplicity made them fair game for any rascally merchant or black marketeer who adventured into their hills; and they lived in an area where wild animals made frequent attacks on their lives and property'[1].

Several ethnographers and anthropologists have described the Kondh way of life in great detail, but while the tribe has been thoroughly studied, their condition has not changed much.

A typical description would begin by how they live. The Kutia Kondh villages are laid out in two long rows of houses in the east–west direction. A small grass-covered gabled roof on wooden posts dedicated to the goddess Deo Pinnu stands on the outskirts of the village. In the middle of the village between the rows of houses, four sacred stones are embedded. These are the *dharni valli*, signifying the throne of Banga Pinnu or Tari Pinnu, the earth goddess. Meriahs would be sacrificed here. Numerous hill gods, one for each hill, form the Kondh pantheon of gods and goddesses.

Many of these traditions are no longer followed but the Kondh women still dress in the distinctively tribal fashion. '... let me describe the wild, remote and devastatingly attractive Kutia Kondhs'[2] is the opening sentence on Kondhs by Verrier Elwin. They are indeed strikingly good-looking. The Kondh woman parts her hair in the middle and, with the help of a ball of string or false hair, arranges the back of her hair into a bun. A brass chain is passed around the top of her head and tied below the bun to secure her coiffure. Bunches of brass rings are passed through a hole in the fold of the helix. All this without a mirror! The lobe of the ear is sometimes decorated with a single brass ring or large brass button. Projecting from the wing of each nostril is a brass pin, and a single brass ring is passed through the septum of her nose. She wears bead necklaces, often patterned in floral designs. More than half of her forearms are lavishly covered with a series of brass or aluminium bracelets.

Sometimes ornamental brass bangles are also worn on the upper arm. There are rings on her toes. An apron is suspended from her neck by the length of a cord. The skirt is knee length.[3]

One of the traditional art forms that continue to be practised is body art. The face of a woman will have stripes and that is something commonly seen as one travels these parts. A woman working on the field will at times put a marigold or hibiscus on her bun. Earlier the women used hairpins made of sambhar bone or porcupine quills; these days they use pins from the market. The dress they wear now is no longer woven by them but purchased from the bazaar. Earlier the Panas would spin their clothes. The lower caste like Panas was meant to weave cloth or engage in any handmade craft.

What is also visibly striking is their body; it is near perfect and many of the women have no embarrassment walking around naked. Surprisingly though, tribal art, unlike Hindu temple art, has very little reference to sexuality. The few examples are tobacco pipes designed as women's areolae and tobacco containers with motifs that represent the nipple and vulva. Sometimes cross beams in Kondh shrines have a pair of breasts but male erotic figures are almost never seen. Cowries, I am told, are an integral part of tribal art but I haven't seen Kondh women wear cowries. The cowrie in various tribal groups in Asia actually represents sexuality But Indian tribals don't see it as a sexual symbol; it is regarded as an attractive decoration and a charm against the evil eye.

One of the most treasured personal belongings of the Kondhs are cases made of a single node of bamboo. But this is nothing to beat the comb, which is integral to Indian antiquity both amongst the tribals as well as non-tribals. Amongst tribal groups combs mean much more than just its function; it is used to titillate the skin of the back and arms. When boys visit girls in the dormitories they bring tobacco tubes and combs as tokens of their love and receive necklaces and bracelets in return. They are the first gifts of wooing. Combs are amongst the most favourite personal items and a must. You will find combs of various shapes and sizes, made of wood, bones or bamboo and carved with geometric designs or human figures.

The dormitories are like love incubators. It is here that the Kondh girl learns the art of making *kapdagonda*, the traditional textile design. The gift of this cloth from a *dhangiri* (unmarried girl) to her *dhangara* (unmarried boy) is a sign of love and bonding. The design is not traced or drawn; they count the threads to achieve the symmetric motifs that appear similar on both sides of the fabric. The geometrical pattern is generally the representation of the Niyamgiri hill and of Creation. For the Dongria Kondhs, Niyam Raja who they believe inhabit Niyamgiri hills is their Creator and for them Niyamgiri is sacred, it's their soul. The forest provides them food and livelihood and they give back by sowing seeds in the forest, a very important part of Kondh life. In April, the various Kondh communities come together to celebrate the Bijun Parab or seed festival where even families who couldn't save any seeds are given seeds to sow. The rules are simple; protection of forest and rivers and common ownership of resources. But this hill rich with bauxite deposit has become synonymous with anti-mine protests in India. The Kondhs won't give it for anything. Their entire identity, they say, resides in this hill.

Kondhs have an attraction for the fantastic and bizarre as seen on wall paintings and masks. Silver ornaments, symbols of the sun and the moon and sometimes just ordinary rupee coins are nailed to the ends of poles and bands of silver are hammered around them. Grotesque images like seen in revelries are visualized in their art forms.

Wall art is not unique to tribals but certain motifs are. The human figure becomes a geometric symbol. Men and animals appear without anatomical details, as if they are in silhouette. Dancers suddenly lose themselves into an abstraction. Breasts are rounded but bird wings fade into rectangles and squares. Fish are drawn with their bones and tortoise in white or red wash. Interestingly, they rarely have images of their gods and goddesses.

The walls of Kondh houses are some five feet high but the roof sometimes comes right down to two feet from the ground, obliterating much of the art which is evanescent. Once made no one looks at them; often the gods send dreams that the art be erased.

In many ways, the tribal areas continue to look much as they did fifty years ago. The most audible and visible differences are cell phones that of course work only when the sky opens up to allow the tribals a window to the world.

Christianity and Communism

The dynamics of the 'red corridor' in Kandhamal are embedded in the differences between castes, tribes and religions. Christianity came to these villages fifty years ago even though the first church by the Baptist Mission Society was set up in the 1920s. According to some records, four tribals were converted in Udagagiri in 1914 on Easter Sunday. They were Bisi, a Pana priest, his wife Lasuri, their son Bondia and his brother-in-law Kusu. Initially, they were ostracized and even water was denied to them, and any outbreaks of disease meant that they must have caused it. But by 1920, there were thirty baptized church members and a church was founded there.

Then Hindu groups came and converted them as well and slowly they started losing their tribal way of life. The killing of missionary Graham Staines and his two sons by right-wing activist Dara Singh in Odisha's Keonjhar district in 1999 marked the rumblings of change. Staines was a Christian missionary who worked with leprosy patients in Odisha for nearly thirty years. He came from Australia in 1965 and opened a leprosy home in Baripada and his work among Adivasis and lepers was well-known.

Allegations of forced conversions were spreading. Right-wing parties had begun to make inroads in bringing the tribals into the Hindu fold; they began clashing with the tribals and Dalit Christians. In 2007, there was a riot between Hindus and Christians.

Then in 2008, the Maoists, till now absent in the region, saw an opportunity to make an impact. They took the side of the Christians and murdered a local VHP leader, triggering horrific anti-Christian riots in Kandhamal. The Maoists came and occupied the space that had opened up but what never arrived was development.

Travels through this corridor take me to Greenbari village where Christians and Hindus live together, trying to forget the past.

Subarna is a Hindu Harijan from the Pana caste, most of whom are landless. She breaks stones for a living just outside the village limits. She gets ₹30 for a basket of stones and she can break about four baskets a day. She wants her children to go to English-medium schools.

Tripura Nayak, a labourer, says that the Church helps them. In these villages, one can witness the liberation theology, a curious mix of Christian options for the poor and Marxist philosophy that preaches the need for social change; it is a doctrine that suits the communist charter but sits uneasily next to the left's anti-religion position.

Meeran just wants rotis and she doesn't care who provides that, Maoists or Christians or Hindus. Though they are hesitant to articulate the fact, what they are essentially saying is that in the absence of government and administration, they are willing to listen to anybody who comes and helps them, and that would include the Maoists.

While agreeing that many of their cadres come from the Christian community, the Maoists disagree that there is any collusion. The Maoist commander of this area admits his cadres are mostly Christians: 'The majority of the people here are Christians. People and priests favour our movement so in that sense they are sympathetic to our movement. Another thing is that when we started we approached people and told them that the fascist forces will rise so the Christians, Muslims and minorities should join the revolutionary movement or else they can't survive – this was our campaign. We supported the people's movement. We organized people in a militia to counter the Hindu fascist offensive.'

The Maoist commander who spoke to me, claims he has always been sceptical of the future of the Maoist movement because it is laden with too many contradictions. 'If the party actually looks at the real situation of the country, not just the forests and rural areas but the vast majority of people in urban centres and working class, students, intelligentsia, youth, if we can organize them, only then it is possible, not just inside the forests with tribals.'

So the 'tribal militancy' with which the movement began seems to have gone nowhere. For the time being the idea of a revolution seems remote even in Kandhamal.

Maoist Medicines

Unlike most Maoist areas in India, Kandhamal has no mines, no big manufacturing units. It has a lot of turmeric though, and apparently one of the best in India, though this is a claim I have heard several other places make. Hence, there is no visible face-off between industrial inroads and tribal rights, unlike in, for example, Jagatsinghpur and Kalahandi districts, where Maoists are said to be backing tribal interests against steel and mining giants Posco and Vendanta.

Here, in Kandhamal, the ground they walk on is starkly poor and grossly underdeveloped, allowing parallel forces like the Maoists to take over.

But what exactly is a Maoist territory? Unlike a typical conflict zone, there is no apparent presence of the militia or any sustained level of disturbance here. One may not notice any mass movement or protest marches here. These areas around Daringbari are not really 'liberated zones' but the villages either have some amount of sympathy or the Maoist diktat runs in the areas.

At least fourteen gram panchayats in this district are under Maoist influence. Sirkabarga is one of them.

Nilandri Muthamajhi, the sarpanch of Sirkabarga (in 2012), is a soft-spoken lady and an unlikely candidate to oversee the problems of around 3,500 people but we are told that she is in charge. She, however, wouldn't speak on the Maoists and says she has heard of them but has never come across one.

Nilandri and her villagers have very basic issues that they want addressed and they don't care who sorts them out: 'Our main problem is road communication. No schools, no anganwadi centres, no potable water, no health service and I think since Independence no government officer has ever visited us.' They know this visit by journalists too will not yield any results.

Tamba Muthamajhi, a former sarpanch, says nothing has changed here in the last sixty-five years. When the missionaries arrived about fifty years ago, they converted to Christianity in the hope of a better life.

At the entry to the village is a fairly big essential commodity shop, unusual for such a remote village. It serves *kakra* (made of flour with coconut filling and fried) and *gulgula* (balls of flour and sugar or jaggery and fried) as morning snacks and though there aren't many customers, the kitchen is bustling with activity. The entire family is engaged in preparing the food. A few villagers hang around perhaps waiting for more to join in the morning's discussion.

There are no graffiti or martyrs' tombs that one finds in other Maoist areas. No sign of any 'revolution'. Not a single banner or signboard that is visible in many other Maoist zones. The area, however, has landmines, we have been told. No wonder government vehicles refuse to enter.

Beyond the *gulgula* snack shop is Borangia village. We are informed that this is another Maoist-influenced area but again there is nothing that stands out in the daily lives of people. Villagers are celebrating the birth of a child; it's the twenty-first day when they have a ceremony and they have hired a generator set to play music while the feast is on. Two adjacent verandahs are busy with the food preparation. Vegetables and fruits are on the menu. The guest list includes the entire village. Local songs are already blaring in the hot morning air; they have a collection of Hindi songs too. There is no ban on popular Indian culture. The Maoists are confused about whether this would affect the 'indigenous' traditions; so far they have stayed away from commenting on it.

Most houses in this village are decorated with paintings of Jesus and Mary. There are two houses where the Indian flag and the Indian map is elaborately detailed indicating all the states of the country. There are paintings of children going to school and the alphabet's first few letters are inscribed in bold. House painting comes very naturally to the tribals but here a lot of the painting is to do with educating children.

The music from the celebration fades as the road leads from paddy fields to the forests to a clearing. A school has stood here for the last ten years but has never been fully functional. All the students are huddled into one classroom because of the lack of teachers. It has just two classrooms for five standards so at a time students of two or three standards are taught together. But that is only when a teacher is available. It is a residential school though the hostel dormitories barely qualify to house children. The warden expresses concern about the safety of the girl students who he fears can be exploited or trafficked.

There is just one teacher who goes on leave and doesn't return for days. The students go to the sarpanch or the government officer of the village block with their complaints but nobody listens. When asked why they don't complain to the 'Maobadis' or Maoists, they feign ignorance and ask, 'Who are the Maobadis?' This is rehearsed speech and they play it to perfection. There is no public allegiance to the Maoists and the secrecy is strictly maintained.

As one travels further into what is perceived as the Maoist heartland one realizes that these are roads hardly travelled and that is because there aren't any roads. Many years ago missionaries came, social workers come now, but the government is conspicuous by its absence. In fact, Kailash Dandapat, of the NGO Jagruti, is the only person who comes here in his red jeep and this particular vehicle is the only one allowed to enter by the people whose diktat runs here. It is just a coincidence that the colour is red!

But how come he is allowed where others are not? Dandapat claims it is transparent work that gives him a passport to the restricted zone.

It appears that the government has been trying to push for development but Maoists scuttle it. Dandapat disagrees, reiterating that honest and transparent work is appreciated. But he gets candid when asked about questioning the Maoists. He says one must not challenge their activities or diktats. The invisible authority of the Maoists is felt very strongly in these parts.

It doesn't require any great insight to understand why these villages of the 'red corridor' of Odisha, also identified as tribal areas, have such stark poverty. Despite such large landholdings these people simply don't have enough to eat. Besides the fact that no development programmes can be initiated here, food is scarce also because there are no irrigation schemes. Here what the people have done is collected money to create an embankment to irrigate the fields. At Sirkabarga, around 400 families have sold cattle and land and raised seven lakhs to construct a dam. But one look and you know it will be washed away in the coming monsoon.

So, what are the Maoists doing for the people they claim to be championing?

The Maoist commander tells me that at 'this stage of the movement the responsibility is on the state. When we try to take up development the state represses people and runs after us, so it's not possible to do any development work. Destruction is first and then construction. For example, we were bringing large amounts of medicines for village health centres but the police started arresting people who had medicines with them, saying they had Maoist medicines. If we made wells villagers were arrested, with the cops saying, 'Maoists came and dug wells for you.' The state is not working for any development. They are aware of the problem but they have not done anything since Independence. The government has been aware for long about what we are demanding. What we are demanding is completely legitimate.'

Back in 1974, Prime Minister Indira Gandhi had written to the home minister about tribal rights (see Annexure 1). Strangely enough, her memo has exactly the same points that the Maoists today demand for the tribals. She observed that there was a 'growing unrest' among tribals across the country and dealt in great detail with issues like land alienation, excise policy, forest policy, licensing of major projects like mining and quality of administration. She even raised the problem of how a government posting in a tribal area is regarded as 'punishment posting'. With so much of understanding of tribal affairs why did the state allow these areas to fester under deprivation and exploitation?

Even in 2015, when the High Level Committee Report on Adivasis was released, the summary was uncannily the same as 1974, with the exception that the role of left-wing extremism (LWE) or Maoists has now entered the picture.[4] Today the Adivasi areas are viewed through the lens of Maoism. It talks of how there has been a subversion of the law by both government and corporations, of the trust deficit that helped the Maoists to enter and claim allegiance of the tribals to protect their interests.

There have been eight committees and commissions[5] set up by the government so far to look into tribal issues but their condition has been as abysmal as ever – they are amongst the most illiterate, live below the poverty line and suffer from extremely poor health. Today, they face massive displacement due to loss of livelihood and also due to dam construction. India is easily the largest dam builder in the world displacing some twenty to fifty million people, the majority of them being tribals.

Liberated Zone in Odisha

The Rumblings: 1960s

The Maoist entry into Kandhamal has been rather recent. The stronghold has always been towards the south, around areas like Koraput and Malkangiri.

The place is no stranger to rebellions: the Gudem Rampa rebellion of 1822–24 in Vishakapatnam and Godavari districts of Andhra Pradesh led by Alluri Sita Rama Raju took the British two years to put down. That battle had spilled over to Koraput. The Telengana peasants' revolt started in 1946 and lasted five years. Given Telengana is not very far, the revolt spread to neighbouring areas like Koraput as well.

Koraput resembles the letter Y with Kalahandi and Raipur districts to its north, Bastar to its west, Srikakulam and Ganjam districts to its east, and Khamman, East Godavari and Vishakapatanam to its south. Strategically this has been the 'Maoist-liberated' zone for decades, with overlapping state borders of Jharkhand, Odisha, Chhattisgarh and Andhra Pradesh.

By the late 1960s, Calcutta was flooded with Naxal literature and the rumblings were felt in some other states.

Students started dropping out from colleges, 'rich' men were targeted and 'class enemies' were attacked. While Charu Majumdar led the Naxalite rebellion in Bengal, the epicenter, with Kanu Sanyal as the architect of the armed uprising, communist leaders like Nagabhushan Patnaik and Gananath Patro provided leadership in Odisha. Charu Majumdar's call to 'liberate' the countryside had become an anthem for students: 'So the first aim and duty of the peasant movement today is to destroy the state machinery. What according to us is a liberated area? We shall call the peasant area a liberated area from where we have to able to oust the class enemies.'

Patnaik was already working with Adivasis in Malkangiri and workers in Balimela when he was arrested in 1966. A lawyer born to a zamindar's family, he rebelled against his father's feudal attitude. He had joined the All India Students Federation and campaigned against the smuggling of rice across the Andhra–Odisha border. He would lie down on the path of the bullock carts to block the passage of the rice.

On 23 January 1969, a secret meeting was held at D. B. M. Patnaik's house at Kapilapur in Gunupur to plan an attack on all the rich people of the subdivision.[6] The tribal villagers were told that the landlords and moneylenders were 'two-legged tigers' sucking their blood for generations and deserved punishment. But the plan failed.

By February 1969, thirty-two cells of communist revolutionaries were active in the forest areas of Gunupur subdivision in Koraput, revealed the Odisha chief minister R. N. Singh Deo in the state assembly[7]. The Adivasis, he said, were organizing themselves to seize property of the moneylenders and landlords. Their target would be the police.

Such were the beginnings of Maoist activity appropriating the issue of tribal rights of the region.

The 'Cut-Off Area': 2011

As one drives from Bhubaneswar to Koraput, the sharp contrast of the road conditions between Odisha and Andhra Pradesh is what strikes an outsider. This contrast is almost symbolic of other state machinery as well – for example, the anti-Maoist operation.

Koraput is a small and almost forgotten town, like many district headquarters in the country. But not quite. The district of the same name is where Hindustan Aeronautics Ltd has its engine division and the National Aluminium Company has been extracting bauxite for a long time. Its rich mineral deposits are well known.

It is the month of April and the evenings are still pleasant. The local newspaper headline says a big Maoist attack is expected following the arrest of one of its leaders, Gasi (Khatru Chedda Bhusanam), who cannot even recall how many people he has killed in his militant career. But the entry gate to the office of the district superintendent of police (SP) in the heart of the town where Gasi is in custody has no one to check visitors. I find my way right to the officer's door. Incidentally, one of the biggest and most daring armoury loots by the Maoists was carried out in this district on 6 February 2004. The absence of security across the district now declared Maoist-affected is peculiar.

As one hits the narrow state highways they look more like garden paths and certainly an impediment for the movement of security forces. For several kilometres, which could stretch to hundreds, there is virtually no movement of any security forces.

The township of Narayapatna is volatile with a lot of unrest following large-scale arrests of a people's movement, the Chasi Muliya Adivasi Sangha (CMAS), partially subverted into a Maoist front. BSF personnel are patrolling the town in motorcycles, but a little distance away their camp looks tentative. It is Ram Navami, so orange squash is being offered to the rare visitor crossing the barricade. Bhaliaput, the village beyond the camp, is deserted because the men escape to the hills during the day and return by night when nobody will venture to patrol these areas. In another direction, the villagers of Dumsil have dug up the road in two places to counter any police movement. But where are the security forces? Partly, the answer lies in the fact that since 1976 no direct recruitment of DSP-ranked police officers has taken place in the state. The strength of the state cadre is 188, of whom only seventy-eight are physically available. So this acute crisis in the police force accounts for the absence of deployment.

The road to Malkangiri is unusually quiet, broken only by the regular potholes of the state highway. It is a nondescript town that doesn't usually excite a newcomer. The news of the high-profile abduction of its Collector, Vineel Krishna, now on leave, is the town's latest introduction[8]. His colleague, the district's police chief, says that beyond 20 kilometres of his office his control ends. In reality, his control perhaps doesn't exist at all. He admits that in many places the only outsiders the villagers have ever met are the Maoists, given the complete absence of state administrative personnel.

The marks of a 'liberated' zone are more pronounced and visible as one enters Chitrakonda in the same district. A dam was built here some forty years ago to supply water to the Balimela hydro project but for most villagers this is literally a 'cut-off' area as is popularly known because of the river, hills and forests cutting it off from any developmental projects or even the nearest town. The remoteness and inaccessibility provides the Maoists a safe haven. The Maoist 'liberated zone' begins here with no government control whatsoever. Three-storey concrete tombs painted in red with the martyr's name below a hammer and sickle dot the arid landscape. The sizes vary according to hierarchy. Bus stations bear the Maoist imprint and even a welcome signpost is clearly visible. The busy office of a paper mill has been running without a glitch in the middle of all this and so is the major ore plant of Essar Steel.

Though the movement of Maoist cadres is apparent, I move ahead towards the Chitrakonda reservoir where thirty-six Greyhound police personnel were killed in an ambush in June 2008. The Greyhound force was raised in Andhra Pradesh as an anti-Maoist crack force. They were returning after an unsuccessful three-day combing operation in a boat when the Maoist guerillas started firing. Just the previous year, eleven special police personnel were killed here. The boatman refuses to take me across, claiming that 200 Maoist cadres have descended on the other side and, without their permission, I cannot be taken. Meetings are being held. Apparently, a big leader has arrived. It was from there that the Collector was abducted and later released against an alleged ransom.

Across the lake, Comrade Ganapathy, the general secretary of CPI (Maoist), addresses a crowd. On such occasions, every villager must attend even if it means losing a day's work. Ganapathy is trying hard to motivate the cadres and sympathizers, highlighting the party's successes.

'In the past three and a half years, in many areas of our country a deluge of mass struggles erupted under our party's leadership. Especially in Dandakaranya, Bihar, West Bengal, Odisha, Maharashtra and Andhra Pradesh, people participated on a large scale in the struggles against the loot of their resources by the Indian and foreign corporations and particularly against the displacement of Adivasis. Though the Indian ruling class formed goonda gangs like Salwa Judum, Sendra, Nagarik, Suraksha Samiti and Harmad Bahini, and perpetrated terrible violence and atrocities on the people, they fought bravely under our party's leadership and with the support of our PLGA [People's Liberation Guerrilla Army]. In Kalinaganagar, Singur, Nandigram, Lalgarh, Narayanpatna, Dumka, Polavaram, Lohandiguda, Raoghat, Pallamad and many other places people mobilized on a large scale and participated in struggles. Nandigram, Lalgarh and Narayanpatna came to the fore as new models of mass struggles. In the various programmes we took up on political issues, we mobilized lakhs of people.'

Ganapathy is acutely aware that mass support is eroding with the government's Green Hunt and is therefore stressing how people have been participating in their programmes.

'In the past three and a half years, the guerilla warfare has intensified and is continuing at a higher level. Our people's guerillas conducted valiant attacks on the police, paramilitary and commando forces that are resorting to endless atrocities and violence and massacring people to further the interests of the exploiting classes. Our guerillas eliminated hundreds of mercenary troops and seized hundreds of modern weapons and ammunition and improved our armoury.'

Villagers from the entire block have now gathered around this high security zone to listen to the leader. He only repeats the obvious to the exhausted villagers who are not in the least interested but the command is to continue sitting there. For years now the Maoists have been uttering the same words, phrases, but very few have been able to question them. Ganapathy now turns towards the failures.

'As we had lost leadership forces in the enemy attack we faced serious losses. After completion of our party Congress, a considerable number of our Central Committee members were caught by the enemy and were either killed in fake encounters or put in jails. This is the very big hindrance we are facing in achieving our goals. No doubt, this would have a grave impact on the Indian revolution. Due to the severe offensive of the enemy and our failure in understanding it properly, formulating proper counter tactics and implementing them, we were weakened in some areas and we retreated in some areas.'

During May 2009 to July 2010, eight top leaders including Cherukuri Rajkumar, known as Azad, have either been caught or killed.

'Comrade Azad was leading the entire urban movement on behalf of our Central Committee and was also looking after political propaganda, party periodicals, party education, etc. In July Azad was to go to Dandakaranya. He and a journalist, Hemchand, were travelling when they were caught and taken to the Adilabad forests and killed the same night. Both their bodies were thrown in the Jogapur forests in the Wankidi mandal of Adilabad district and a fake encounter story was concocted as always. Former Union Home Secretary G. K. Pillai, former police chief Prakash Singh and Union Home Secretary Chidambaram and such people are saying that we would fall into line only if pressure is built up. They are living in a fool's paradise.'

Back in Delhi the Home Secretary of the central government, G. K. Pillai is already talking about the gains.

'Specialized training, intelligence-based operations, I must say, are getting us results. We have arrested two politburo members in the last six months. We have arrested four central committee members, a state committee member, Deepak Talgu, in West Bengal and we are slowly starting to get that intelligence. People are going to come and give information only when they feel the government is going to stay there.'[9]

The Maoist methodology, as the government perceives it, is to initially gain control of base areas which they would like to develop as liberated zones. They typically operate in administrative vacuums. The Home Secretary acknowledges the fact that government policies encourage the Maoist stranglehold.

'There are some areas in Malkangiri area. Many of you may not know that as a result of a dam which came up in the late 1960s, there are more than 141 villages which got isolated. Believe me if I say today that many people will be surprised those 141 villages have not been seen by anybody in either the state or central government since 1969. Nobody has ever gone to them. There is not a single road, there is no BDO, no village officer, but we know they exist because the Maoists came there, became their friends, indoctrinated them.'

The government may have been moving ahead but they are far from hitting the real fighting force of the Maoists. The fighting has been going on with the lower levels, such as village supporters. The real armed cadres have not been tracked yet. Their training is done by former members of the army and paramilitary forces. Every attack undergoes a postmortem and that is a very professional way of going about things. Like military doctrines they circulate bulletins of lessons learned.

The government thinks the only way to approach this situation is to empower the police force. But with three lakh vacancies, it is a war already lost. Odisha has just above 100 policemen against a population of a lakh. Bihar's ratio of police to a lakh population is 56 and that is one-fourth of what should be. The normal range is 220 policemen to a lakh population.

The deficiencies are so glaring that it may take much more than just governance. In west Midnapore district in Bengal which is affected by Maoists, there were 4,000 vacancies for teachers in 2012. One district in Bihar had only three MBBS doctors. The situation in tribal districts of Odisha is worse.

If the use of force is going to be the one and only approach, then the government is bound to lose this war again and again. Force may help manage the level of violence but cannot address the grievances on which the Maoists will piggyback and run their writ.

Adivasi Resistance and Naxalbari

Sidhu, Kanhu, Chand, Bhairab

The Adivasi resistance against land usurpation and taxation goes back centuries. There was widespread discontent amongst the tribals of Bengal, Bihar and Odisha under British rule. Midnapore witnessed two waves of violence: the Chuar rebellion of 1799–1800 and the Bhumij revolt of 1832–33. In the early nineteenth century, the tribal people of Midnapore and Singhbhum fought the British with classic guerilla tactics: 'the rebels were never to be completely suppressed so long as they could take refuge in the wilds and vastness to the west … and pounce down when the opportunity offered.'[10] 'It is seldom that any party can take them by surprise, they get notice of our approach, they separate and conceal themselves in the holes and caverns of thick jungles until our return toward camp, when they creep out to take a sly shot at the rear column.'[11]

Though the rebellion was suppressed, within three decades the oppressive impact of British land revenue policies precipitated another uprising among the Bhumij tribals of the same area.

As shifting cultivators, the Santhals followed the slash and burn technique, and slowly and steadily had to encroach upon the plains from their forests. Without advanced agricultural methods, their land productivity was low. They could not pay the high rents on land owned by zamindars. The British land revenue system left the Santhals with virtually nothing. In British records one can find physician, botanist and surveyor Francis Buchanan Hamilton's account indicating how moneylenders charged interest at the rate of 100 per cent for their food and nearly 150 per cent for their seed. So, when their crops were ready, little to nothing remained for themselves.

The accounts of British civil servants as found in books such as W. W. Hunter's *The Annals of Rural Bengal* the Santhal condition is apparent:

> In the administration of the Santhal settlement, everything that cost money without bringing in a tangible return was avoided. Nothing was spent in obtaining the knowledge of the people. The superintendent was pre-eminently a practical man; and so it fell out that, early in 1855 the most peaceful province in the empire became the scene of a protracted rebellion, without any one being able to give either warning or explanation. Many of the Santhals had no land or crop to pledge for their little debts. If a man of this class required a few shillings to bury his father, he went to the Hindu usurer for it; having so security to offer except his manual labour and that of his children, he bound over himself and family as slaves till the loan should be repaid.[12]

Destruction of forests further forced Santhals to migrate to other districts, and even as far as Bihar's Dumka subdivision. The areas inhabited by them came to be known as Damin-i-koh. Their territory, which spread from Cuttak across Manbhum, Chota Nagpur, Hazaribagh, Palamow, to Rewah now moved to Damin-i-koh. By 1851, there were 82,795 Santhals in the Damin-i-koh's 1473 villages, according to some accounts. They were extorted and exploited and most families found themselves in inextricable debt.

> Without the slightest warning the poor husbandman's buffaloes, cows and little homestead were sold, not omitting the brazen household vessels which formed the sole heirloom of the family. Even the cheap iron ornaments, the outward tokens of family respectability among the Santhals were torn from the wife's wrist. Redress was out of question: the court sat in the station perhaps a hundred miles off.[13]

In 1855, some 5,000 Santhals from Birbhum, Bankura, Chotanagpur and Hazaribagh began meeting in Damin-i-koh for the purpose of avenging the treatment inflicted on their people. Four brothers, Sidhu, Kanhu, Chand and Bhairab, embarked on a 'divine mission' to evict all 'foreigners' from their soil and liberate their people from oppression. The rebellion spread to adjoining districts. The ill-prepared British forces were defeated at the battle of Pirpainti with the 'hand-bows' and 'kind of battle axe' the 'rebels' used[14]. But finally, the tribals were crushed, forced from the plains and hounded into the jungles. It was, however, the insurrection of Hul which remains a very important historical marker in Santhal imagination and subaltern studies. The rebellion was political in nature; they did not rebel out of primordial urges, or hunger; their movements were specifically against colonial authority, and the authority of landlords and moneylenders. In 1855, Sidhu declared that he had a divine order to rebel against the British and this is popularly known as the Hul Rebellion. Though most of the accounts are what historian Ranajit Guha says 'prose of counter-insurgency, what is evident is that the Santhals mobilized against a system where tribal access to land was made tenuous and dependent on a number of authorities who extorted them for what was traditionally theirs.'

In the Census Report of 1872, the total number of 'Sonthals' returned were 9,23,532, of whom half were in the Sonthal Parganas south of Bhagalpur division. They inhabited a tract about 560 kilometres in length from the Ganges in Bhagalpur to the Baitarni river in Odisha. But slowly as the forests were being encroached the Santhals started migrating.

Rebellions Continue

The migration of Santhals continued and when Terai was annexed from Sikkim, the British contracted Santhals to work mainly in the tea gardens of North Bengal. Not everybody got jobs and moneylenders followed them there as well. The Santhals were easy prey. The ones living outside the tea gardens became sharecroppers and they were the ones involved in the 'peasant rebellion' of Naxalbari in the state of West Bengal. Though there are instances earlier of left-wing involvement in tribal uprisings, this was the moment when the revolution can be said to have lit the fire.

Before the Naxalite movement and even before Tebhaga and Telengana movements, the birth of the Kisan Sabha in 1936 led to the rise of militant Prajamandal movements that often united the tribal and non-tribal rural poor. Niligiri Prajamandal in Odisha raised the questions of minimum wages and standardization of measurements.

North Bengal was one of the centres of the Tebhaga movement in 1946–47, described as 'the outgrowth of left-wing mobilization of rural masses ... the first consciously attempted revolt by a politicized peasantry in Indian history'.[15] It was a peasant movement to retain a two-third share of the produce for themselves and reduce the rent they paid to jotedars.

Artist Somnath Hore chronicled the movement in Rangpur, one of the pockets where the revolt intensified along with Dinajpur, Jalpaiguri and Malda, with his sketches and observations in his diary:

> 19 Dec 1946
> Keshto-da spoke about harvesting the rice. 'You must finish harvesting the rice. Don't wait for others. Just organize yourselves into groups and start. You mustn't store the harvested grain in the jotedar's shed. Keep it in your homes and then distribute it according to the tebhaga principle: two thirds and one third. And insist on a receipt. If a landlord refuses, keep his share of the harvest at your own house or deposit it at the Samiti's stores. Organise volunteer forces, cut branches for lathis, raise banners, pick up your sickles and shout, "We want tebhaga!"'
>
> 20 Dec 1946
> The harvesting was to start this morning ... About a hundred and fifty people had gathered, with virtually everyone carrying a sickle and a lathi. Even children of five or six were carrying sickles or holding up banners. The red flag was raised in the middle of the field. The boundaries were

> indicated with flags. The lathis were planted at one spot and everyone trooped into the field with sickles in hand. The air reverberated with slogans. People broke into song, 'Young red flag's your red salute, O peasant.' The rice was harvested to the rhythm of the song.

It started in November 1946; the state unleashed force on the peasants and on 4 January 1947 the first police firing was recorded, killing Sibram, a landless Santhal peasant, and Samiruddin, also a landless peasant. Though the Santhals remained militant, the movement disintegrated. The police was used to crush it completely but there was a continuity with the Naxal uprising.

Birsa Munda

Besides the Hul Rebellion, in the Santhal imagination Birsa Munda occupies the central role of having led the tribals to what some historians call India's 'first war of independence'.

Though it is apparent that tribal or Adivasi resistance has morphed into the Maoist movement at least in some form, the term 'Adivasi' itself is often not well understood and is contentious. The word has assumed a political connotation of exclusion and tribal rights, their resistance, assertions, protests and movements. The Indian Constitution does not use the term Adivasi, instead refers to Scheduled Tribes or Anusuchit Jana Jati. However, not all Adivasis are Scheduled Tribes.[16] And there are parallel dynamics of tribes, religion and Maoism. Some common markers define these dynamics. Birsa Munda is one such marker and the perception of tribal 'uprising' connects him to the larger narrative of Adivasi rights and resistance.

Adivasi folk songs refer to both Ulihatu and Chalkad as his birthplace though his burial stone is found in Ulihatu.

> O, pray tell me, how far is Chalkad? I shall go slowly.
> Some say, it is eastward, others say it is southward.
> O, I shall go to the South slowly,
> The wild forest is infested with leopards and bears, and they make terrible sounds,
> O, I shall go, together or slowly?
> Birsa's words are pleasing, I too shall go and listen to him.

Birsa was converted to Christianity by the German Mission when he was twelve. He was sent to study at the Mission school in Chaibasa where conversion was mandatory to join the school. The folk songs draw Biblical parallels of his birthplace: a comet or a flag star moved across the sky from Chalkad to Ulihatu; a flag flew on a mountaintop. When he went to school his teacher saw his palm and observed a cross and predicted that he would recover the kingdom one day.

Birsa grew up in abject poverty in a house made of bamboo strips without mud plaster or even a proper roof. He was just like any other Munda child. He started playing the flute and went around with a *tuila* – a one-stringed instrument made from a pumpkin – in his hand and the flute strung to his waist.

Later, following his family, he gave up the German Mission and joined Roman Catholicism before he gave that up too and returned to his own beliefs. He is believed to have walked out of the school and the order to protest his teacher's disparaging remarks against Mundas. By now Birsa had moved home several times and arrived at Bandgaon where he came across a Hindu Vaishnav monk; he adopted the sacred thread and began to smear sandalwood paste on his forehead. Birsa was seen by his followers as the image of Vishnu.

During 1893–94, all wasteland in villages had been converted to protected forests under the Indian Forest Act VII of 1882. Soon he joined an agitation against restrictions imposed upon the traditional rights of the Mundas in the protected forests.

Birsa was already a popular leader by then. He had several love affairs and many marriages that went against Christian beliefs and his own prescription of monogamy. However, this was not unusual in the Munda community. With time Birsa assumed the role of a prophet and people came to see him and listen to him from distant villages.

Birsa was now preaching a new religion but his following and his popularity had been hijacked by the Sardar Agitation to push for their rights. The agitation was triggered by popular disaffection at the restrictions imposed upon the traditional rights of the Mundas in the protected forest. But Birsa had assumed a different avatar and announced that all non-believers would be massacred and called for his followers to be ready with arms. His anger was directed against the police who was harassing him and the influential tribal zamindar of Bandgaon and the headman of Kochang who had defied him.

In 1895, the government arrested Birsa in a midnight operation on elephant back. Birsa had told his people that if the police were to arrest him, he would return to them on the third day and a log of wood would be left behind in his cell in the jail. But three days passed and Birsa did not return. Instead, the Prophet of Chalkad was sentenced to two years of rigorous imprisonment. In despair and fear, his followers reconverted to Christianity to escape the terror of the British government. Though the government congratulated itself on having squashed the uprising, this marked the beginning of a widespread movement.

While in jail some of his followers had started spreading absurd tales of Birsa's prophetic character. Upon his release, his followers returned to him and Birsa started preparing for another uprising.

In the 1892 uprising, there was only a suggestion of suspension of rent to zamindars, holding lands rent-free and reestablishing the Mundas' rights in the forests. They would appoint the Maharaja and rent was paid to him for his maintenance but 'outsiders' did not have any rights, and this new movement wanted to assert that and expel all middlemen and intermediaries. With Birsa and his new religion of Birsaite, the Mundas came under one forum and attacks were launched against the European masters.

Interestingly, as early as 1855, the official correspondence of the British administration had started calling the Mundas insurgents:

> Reports from Afzulpore Thannah, mention that the inhabitants of Baboopore Deolee & Kejoree have their villages which have not as yet, however been plundered by the Sonthals.
>
> Sonthals have again looted 'Rajor' 4 miles from Nungolea thannah suspected to be the same men ...
>
> N.B. I have requested Col. Burney, to order Captn. Gott stationed with a detachment at Nungolea, to make a night march, and if possible surprise these Insurgents number about 600 men.[17]

Birsa spent his last days moving from place to place. Rogoto was where he had his last meeting with the Birsaites, laying down instructions regarding his religion and a code of conduct for his followers. Seven men from neighbouring villages were apparently paid a reward of Rs 500 to capture Birsa.

Birsa knew his end was near but he left a prophecy: 'As long as I do not change this body of earth, you will not be saved. Do not be disappointed. Do not think that I left you in the lurch. I have given you all the weapons, all instruments. You will save yourselves with them.' On another occasion, he said: 'I will turn up one day. I will light the bonfire of the Holi festival in Bundu, Tamar, Singbhum, Keonjhar, Gangapur and Basia.'

Birsa died on 9 June 1900 and slowly the movement died, but the British started looking at land rights, an issue that is at the heart of tribal resistance even today.

Political movements centering on tribal ethnicity based themselves on Birsa. A confidential report by the SP of Ranchi, forty years after Birsa's death, remarked:

> It is a fact that Birsa Munda's name is known throughout this district and outside, largely because of his rebellion and common belief that the establishment of the khuntkatti[18] right was the result of his sacrifice. The local Adivsai leaders consider the advent of Birsa Munda to be the beginning of the aboriginal awakening and trace the subsequent organisations such as Unnati Samaj, Kishan Sabha sponsored by Theble Oraon, Rai Saheb Bandi Ram and other Sabhas managed by respective Indian Christians to be the ultimate outcome of the awakening … There appears to be deep respect for him … The name Birsa Munda undoubtedly stirs them.

Naxalbari: Where It All Began

2014

The Name of a Village
… when my child
Returns from school,
And not finding the name of the village
In his geography map,
Asks me
Why it is not there,
I am frightened
And remain silent.
But I know
This simple word
Of four syllables
Is not just the name of a village,
But the name of the whole country.

– From a Hindi poem by Kumar Vakil[19]

The 'four syllabled' village is Naxalbari.

I have travelled to Naxalbari a number of times but each time I failed to encounter anybody who remembered the 'uprising' or had participated in it. By the time I got some contacts for Kanu Sanyal who lived in Naxalabari, he had taken ill and committed suicide a year later. Thirty-five-year-old Kanu Sanyal, a district council member of the CPI (M), initiated a movement in Naxalbari of forcible occupation of land and the expropriation of hoarded rice and paddy. Between March and May 1967 at least a hundred incidents were reported of farmers occupying land using bows and arrows. The uprising was soon crushed and by mid-1970 the Naxalite rebellion was brought under control using excessive force.

I have a friend, a Santhal from Naxalbari, and hoped he could help me trace the people involved in the struggle. Chacko took me around and we met a few people who tried to think of someone who could tell me what had happened on the day of the 'uprising' or how it all built up. It wasn't easy because nobody really cared about that incident. They didn't even know how the name Naxalbari came into being or what it means.

In search of the Naxalbari of my growing up stories, I was led into a narrow alley of Siliguri town where the CPI (ML) office is located; the entrance is by a well in the dark backyard of a house.

I wanted to hear about the 'movement' from Charu Majumdar's son.

Abhijit Majumdar teaches English literature in a college in Siliguri and is a member of the central committee of the CPI (ML). He sits on a wooden chair, smoking, in a room with a few pictures – one of Charu Majumdar, another of Naxalbari martyrs' tombs and one each of Lenin and Stalin. Tiny cups of tea are served to us. Heaps of propaganda material are piled up all around the room. It could well be an evening from the 1970s, as Abhijit begins to talk:

> You have to go to a place to Hatighisa. Shanti Munda is now old but she will talk. You've visited Kanubabu's place, haven't you? Shanti Munda lives close by, in Sablaldajot. She is the only surviving member of those who participated in the uprising that day in 1967. Babulal Bishwakarma lives in Hochaimulikjot; he was the first martyr. Agnu Toppo is someone you may not be able to track. He was involved in the first rifle-snatching case in Magurjan. There is another surviving Adivasi leader, Khudan Mullick. If you speak to them, they will be able to give you a graphic picture. On 25 May, when the police opened fire killing eleven, there were two tea garden women workers whose families migrated and could never be tracked. They (Shanti and Khundan) would be able to tell you how many Adivasi tea garden workers and Adivasi farmers were involved in the first uprising. How that uprising matches with today's situation is something they will be able to tell you. There are still a few people surviving of those who witnessed the birth of this movement. Soon they will be gone.
>
> Shanti Munda's son-in-law who was her contact has now shifted to Trinamool Congress but she is still active and you can meet her. Agnu Toppo's family would have been great to track simply because when most frontline leaders were incarcerated he carried out an operation without any orders and this is unwritten history, something nobody has ever recorded. Charu Majumdar has written about him.
>
> We forget the preparatory stages of two decades ago from 1967. The communist revolutionaries were busy preparing the ground. In pre-Independence times, since the tea gardens

were called 'estates', they had their own rules and nobody was allowed to enter; they had a mixed sort of demography of indentured labour force brought from the Chotanagpur plateau but they became 'original' inhabitants here. The Adivasis here are very different from the Adivasis of Odisha or other places like south Bengal because they are industrial workers and their livelihood is related to production so organizing them was much easier. At the same time since tea gardens are on land leased out by the government, so what happened here was that non-plantation areas were used as housing … the extra land was perennially cultivated by them, so they were a parallel labour force as well as cultivators. They were not labelled as Adivasis or Rajbonshis, there was no political ideology targeted towards Adivasis. When the communist revolution addressed it (the labourers and peasants), it was to do with food crisis that was worldwide. There is no database of how many Adivasis were part of this because they were not identified as separate participants. Land became the focal point. In the preparatory stages, therefore, the Adivasi was not synonymous with the Naxal movement.

Though the agenda of an industrial workforce is quite different from peasantry, in the revolutionary movement they were not treated separately since most of the workers were peasants too. There were no trade unions. Police repression was significant. It is thus difficult to quantitatively analyse the movement.

Just like the movement of '70s in Presidency College is different from what we see in Jadavpur today, those were different times, the class base was different, the lower middle class was homogenous. Similarly, here there was no sharp class difference. You will find the middle class has always played a role in any revolution. Politics should be brought into the masses from outside, which is the Marxist logic. Within the Marxist theory, the citizen should be able to correlate at least with the bourgeois education system. Today, amongst the Naxals, sharp class differences are more visible; then it was much more natural, not a conscious one ... a dialectical relationship.

Naxalbari today ... ask at the market place about the revolution and people will say they don't even know about it or have only vaguely heard of it. There has been a concerted effort towards this over the last thirty-four years, in writing history books or documentation ... Whatever we may think and would like to imagine, Naxalbari is a relic today; the public perception is that it is a relic. We have to retrace our footsteps or else how do we move ahead?

My father never wrote about Adivasis separately. Sociology is not politics; sociology was brought in to destroy class politics, the Marxists believe. Social scientists started categorizing class politics like habitat, etc. and diffused the politics. That is a different debate altogether. Though Karl Marx was himself a social scientist more than a political person.

Though Majumdar may deny that it was a conscious decision to mobilize the Adivasis, the perception even in the media was that it was a tribal uprising. On 27 May 1967, the editorial in *The Statesman* observed that '... the tribals have been encouraged if not actively led by political workers of the extreme Left of the Left Communist Party ...'

Though the Naxalite leadership was battered and broken after the first burst, the ideology triggered numerous journals, literature and films in colleges and back lanes of Calcutta. In the villages, though, the perceived support the ideology received was actually from the Santhals. The Santhals saw their participation in Naxalite activities as in consonance with their traditional identity and values.

The Naxalites were quick to pick this up and in 1968, the Bihar State Co-ordination Committee of Communist Revolutionaries went so far as to issue a statement: 'Let every Adivasi rise and fight the way the great Birsa, the great Siddu and Kanu fought against the oppressors.'

By 1969, the CPI (ML) had reinvented itself in Bengal and developed a significant underground organization with the tribals. Under Ashim Chatterjee the Bengal–Bihar–Odisha border region committee started organizing the local poor and landless population. In the predominantly Santhal areas of Debra and Gopiballavpur, the Naxalite leadership began to mobilize people. Killings of landlords started and village committees were set up to do away with the credit system and demand that moneylenders write off debts. These methods appealed to the Santhals who joined the movement en masse.

The Midnapore uprising[20] failed but the party opened up a new front in Birbhum district. In mid-1971, they declared the formation of a 'People's Army' and a long march by Santhals was organized in Bolpur carrying rifles and muskets. The economic demands of the tribals rather than the party ideology was the focus. Revolutionary Committees and People's Courts gave the Santhals and Scheduled Castes a taste of power. Parallel and arbitrary institutions of power emerged. Santhal Maoists like Gunadhar Murmu, Jangal Santhal, Leba Chand Tudu and Rabi Manjhi were able to gain leadership status. Just as Mao wooed strategic minorities with promises of autonomy, as the Viet Cong wanted the tribal 'Front Unifie de Lutte de la Race Opprimee', and as the Greek communists collaborated with Macedonian nationals in 1946, similarly the Naxalites sought Santhal alliance. Entire families of Santhals joined the movement; the natural authority of elders became the political and military authority. But each squad had at least one caste Hindu or intellectual Bengali, a pattern that continues to this day where the central committee has caste Hindu intellectuals while the cadres are tribal guerillas.

The Santhals responded to situations of crisis in a variety of ways. They migrated as far as Assam and occasionally they responded with violence. The messianic character of their rebellion is also significant. Sidhu, Kanu, Chand and Bhairab all claimed to have been visited by a Bonga, a supreme diety. Birsa was the prophet. Then Bhagrit started the Kherwar movement that became a socio-religious movement rather than a political one.[21]

Throughout the course of their migration and revolt, they maintained a proud sense of their militant tribal history through songs sung even today.

> *Sindhu kanu ghyrghure upare/* Sindhu Kanu on a chariot
> *Chand Bhairab ghorai/* Chand Bhairab on a horse
> *Dekh sere Chand Bhairab/* See them Chand and Bhairab
> *Ghorai Bhairab mulin mulin/* On horseback, Bhairab forward, forward
>
> Sindhu, why are you bathed in blood?
> Kanu, why do you cry revolt, revolt?
> For our brothers, we have bathed in blood
> For the trader thieves
> Have robbed us of our land.

It was in this revolutionary cultural context that 'Santhal Naxalism' found its roots. Pradip Banerjee, a CPI (ML) leader, once said, 'When we went to the Santhals we would emphasize their heroes Sindhu and Kanu and speak of their militant legacy. We told them that Sindhu and Kanu were our predecessors and the "New Democracy" was no different from what they fought for.' Santhali tunes became the source of Naxalite revolutionary songs.

> Sindhu Kanu Chand Bhairab
> Had started the revolt
> Mao Tsetung Charu Majumdar
> Will finish the revolt

They started giving new meaning to the popular Santhal tunes, developing them on themes such as the Hul rebellion of 1855, just like the nineteenth Christian missionaries had done when converting them to Christianity.

Jal, Jungle, Jameen: 2014

PRADEEP

Across the border in Jharkhand is Gumla, under the control of the CPI(Maoist). Villagers extend sympathy to the 'party' for the wretched socio-economic conditions even in 2014.

Pradeep, an elderly Oraon tribal, explains the dynamics of the tribals vis-à-vis the Maoists: 'As our tribal saying goes, "Jal, Jungle, Jameen" – our lives are primarily dependent on these three things. For sustaining livelihoods, people here are generally engaged in agricultural work. With regard to "Jungle", our dependency has decreased in the recent times, given the ongoing high rate of deforestation; earlier, selling

Mahua flowers was a chief economic activity. To add to this, the agricultural produce is often not enough, forcing people to migrate to urban centres in search of some labour jobs. Hundreds of families have become women headed because the men go out and now even the women are leaving for work. Villages are becoming deserted. Most of our people here have failed to adapt to new agricultural techniques so their yield is lower than others. And who is interested in agriculture these days? Not the youth. After completing their 10th standard, these young boys often move to Delhi or Punjab or even the south of India in search of labour jobs.'

The tribals here are better off today and the tribal–non-tribal face-off is not that rough. The tribals are aware of discrimination and wouldn't take it lying down. Neither is untouchability practised any longer.

'The government may have tried to raise our living standards but everyone agrees they have no imagination or inclination; for example, the government provided loans but people couldn't pay back so the enterprises failed. Vocational training was being provided but nobody was interested here. I think the problem is that the people here don't trust the government with welfare schemes. Most of the schemes are merely reported on papers. There is a lot of tokenism that has been going on.

'The government schemes are more likely to harm the social fabric. The Public Distribution System has converted farmers who earlier laboured hard on farms into idle villagers. Now, they merely live off the PDS grains, knowing that they can avail almost free food grains without toiling on their farms. Similar is the government's education policy. These policies prohibit teachers from failing anyone, can you imagine this? Thus, there is a complete lack of interest in studying. Students passing out from these villages are not competent enough to sit for competitive examinations. There's too much of unemployment, and the government has done little to improve things for the tribal community.'

'Government figures, the numbers they come up with, will tell you a different story – that conditions have improved. Yes, some conditions are better but most of the improvements are limited to the non-tribal population in these areas. They benefit the most from government schemes, irrespective of the fact that they don't need it. PDS cards, for example, are used by the wealthy. Same goes for the Indira Awas Yojana. There's too much of corruption involved, and the tribals or most of us don't know to work around such corrupt officials. This is not to suggest that tribals are all innocent; many tribal youths have taken up the role of middlemen. The other government policies like PDS are also corrupt. They give away only 20 kilos instead of 30 kilos, and that too at double the price. Much of MNREGA's work is limited to paper only; payment delays are often more than six months.'

The one thing that villagers feel has changed for the better is the police attitude and that is almost entirely due to the Maoists. 'A few years back, the police would beat up and file false cases against us; the police would later demand bribes for clearing the case. The conditions were such that we would run away on seeing the police. When the Maoists came into these areas, the police forces realized the need for the people's support. Their treatment of the people slowly improved.'

'With increasing Maoist domination the police decreased patrolling; they fear that the Maoists might come after their arms and ammunition. A year and a half back, the Maoists had ambushed a jeep of police officials and killed all of them. The incident took place in the middle of the market during the daytime. There were six or seven policemen inside the jeep. The Maoists first surrounded the vehicle and started shooting one by one.' When this was happening, they told Pradeep and his friends – people who were shopping – to maintain a distance so that they don't get caught in the crossfire.

'Even when someone dies in this area, the police hardly come to investigate the case or take the body in their custody; they tell the family members to bring the dead bodies to the police station on their own. Also, most of the criminal cases are being handled or resolved at the gram sabha level; hence there is very little involvement of the police in village matters.'

Both police and administrative officials have minimum presence in this area. The government projects are carried out through contractors, who pay the Maoists and other parties a fixed percentage.

'The administrative officials are afraid for the same reason. Some days after the shooting incident, they bombed the block office here. They claimed that all the government servants working there were corrupt and would ask for bribes to get anything done. They say they target only the corrupt. But many of these things are propaganda they themselves spread, so it is difficult for someone to ascertain who is corrupt and who isn't.'

'When the Maoists first came to this place, they fought against the injustices being committed against the tribals. They would only attack landlords who persecuted the tribals. However, in recent times, things have seen a complete turnaround. Their motive now seems to be to prevent security forces from coming to these areas; that's all they are concerned about. They have stalled almost all the development projects in the area. There's an environment of fear among the people. You have to listen to their commands. When a meeting is called, everyone has to attend it. People just nod along with whatever the Maoists say, for the fear of being noticed in a way that may make him/her a suspect. A village head was beaten up because the party alleged that he was speaking against the party. Earlier, the party members would conduct a proper investigation and only then did they announce the verdicts. Now they are desperate.'

'The most confusing thing in these areas is there's no clarity on who belongs to which group. Every faction has to be attended seriously. There are several small groups in the area, many of which work in the name of the Maoists. If the Maoists come to know about them, they mostly end up six inches short. However, for us commoners, they appear the same. Many of the small groups – might be that the MCC (Maoist Communist Centre) is involved too – are engaged in extorting money from the residents, especially teachers and retired military personnel.'

'When it comes to recruitment, they sometimes forcibly take away people. The Maoists had earlier made a demand of two to three recruits from every village. This is one of the primary reasons why many youths have migrated to urban centres for good. Many a time, people are looted in broad daylight. People are even afraid of travelling; the Maoists often ask for people's vehicles if someone has one. You cannot complain to the police; if they come to know about it, they will kill you.'

'People are afraid of all the factions. One cannot afford to offend them, let alone speak against them. Some months back, a teacher had objected to them coming to the school during class hours; some of the armed members had come to the school during class hours and were roaming around the school corridors, to which the teacher had objected. They caught the teacher by his neck in front of the class and warned him to not make any such comments.'

'The Maoists mostly come to villages during the night, for food. They never demand any particular food but eat whatever they are being served. Sometimes, they even pay the people for food. But one hardly gets to hear about them helping any villager in times of need. One doubts they even have any money themselves. The leaders, the villagers think, must be making a lot of money.'

'I don't think they have done anything yet to benefit the community. Sometime back, they threatened a school principal here, asking him to improve school results, but that's all. They have tried doing this for decades. The one thing is that they never mistreat women. They would themselves never tease or trouble a girl, nor will they allow others to do it. One is not sure what they do to their own women. But they will even kill their own member if he is found to have raped a woman. The other thing that they are apparently very serious about is the felling of trees. They have given very strict instructions to the villagers to not cut trees. They often say that the cutting down of jungles is detrimental to their survival. Someone found cutting a tree is generally beaten up by the members. On the alcohol issue, no, they are not too strict here. They haven't issued any public warnings against alcohol sellers or drinkers.'

RONALD

We travel to the neighbouring village that cannot be named for obvious reasons, where we meet Ronald who agrees with his elder neighbour on most aspects but has stronger support for the Maoists.

'People here are primarily dependent on agriculture, but that is not enough to sustain ourselves. There are no employment opportunities. Such conditions have forced many like me to migrate to other places in search of jobs. I am here on leave now. Such conditions have also led to human trafficking in these areas; middlemen, often promising hope of a better life, take away people, especially girls. Everyone knows of the large number of our tribal girls working in Delhi and other cities. Most have been trafficked. The guardians too are hardly concerned. They are glad that the children are being taken care of. So many times, girls migrate voluntarily for they see no opportunities in these areas, and also because of the drinking problems in most families. Our society has become alcoholic.'

'The government has nothing to improve the living conditions of the people here or to alleviate any of our basic problems. Anti-trafficking mechanisms in fact allow the middlemen to thrive and the law is of little use. There is no enforcement.'

'When it comes to education, the government agencies are highly corrupt. Every year, they get some money to take the students out for some excursion, for the purpose of exposure; however, they never do that. The only good schools are some missionary schools that are almost 7-8 kilometres from here. How can we expect our children to have better future if they are not properly educated?'

'All the government schemes meant for us, the tribals, are either taken away or delayed. MNREGA related payments are always delayed; several of their works too have not been completed. There are no surveys being conducted for BPL cards, and yet they have BPL cards being distributed to so many who do not qualify. The officials never visit us here.'

'The attitude of the police has changed slightly but they are still removed from the people. Though the forces are more active, the party is also getting stronger. The incident of party members blowing up the block office was done at a time when people thought that the party's strength had decreased. They blasted the office in the early hours of the morning. Hours before that, sometime close to midnight, they had attacked the police station; they kept firing at the police station for more than two or three hours. The sub-inspector there happened to be somewhat lucky to have held on to the beleaguered post. The villagers heard the firing throughout the night. After they failed to take over the police station, on their way back, they blasted the block office.'

'The Maoists too have changed their strategy after the police increased their presence in these areas. Earlier, there was too much bloodshed and beheading if villagers were suspected of being police informers. That has come down now.'

'Maoists don't trouble us unnecessarily. Their ideology seems people-centric. Whenever there are disputes or conflicts in the villages, they resolve the dispute only if the villagers seek their help. They don't interfere in village matters on their own. They also protect people from bullies or anti-social elements. In our village, there was a criminal who had become a nuisance for everyone. He would trouble everyone, exert forcible influence in the decision-making of villages, and was involved in looting people. Anyone new travelling in these areas was not safe. When the Maoists came to know about this problem, they killed this guy. The incidents of robbery have stopped since then. So the kangaroo court and vigilante justice is very much in place.'

'They completely stopped the sale of alcohol in these areas. If teachers don't show up in school on time, the party members call them and ask them to explain why they have been absent. The only thing that they ask is providing food for their members; the villagers don't have any problem with that. They eat whatever they are offered.'

'They have completely banned the cutting of trees. Yes, they did go extreme on this, many years ago. About fifteen or twenty years back, there was this lady who would cut trees every day. The party members cautioned her several times, may be more than a hundred times, but she did not listen to them and kept on chopping trees. This lady was a single mother; her child was around one or two years old. The party members, as punishment, killed her child, cutting him into two, before the woman, and told her this was how they felt when she cut trees. However, the party members are no more into any such extreme activities of unnecessary violence. They are now closer to us.'

'In recent times, however, they are more into explaining their ideology to people and listening to their grievances. They keep talking about the Marxist-Leninist ideology. However, this does not mean that they have gone soft on their commands. The party's orders have to be followed, come what may. For example, when they call for a meeting, it's necessary for everyone to attend.'

'Yes, I was cautioned once a few days back. I was having lunch at my place when an armed cadre, about twelve or thirteen years old, came to my home, and asked me to be present for the meeting; he also told me that if I don't attend, I would get beaten by a rifle's butt.'

'So we had this letter from the party, asking us to attend the meeting at a given place. When we reached there, there were already people from several other villages. Once everyone was there, they asked us to present the problems people faced in their daily lives. One from every village was supposed to speak about the problems; my village members asked me to present the problems, which I reluctantly did while withholding plenty of information. After that, the party members gave us a detailed account of how we didn't express all our problems. They told us about the problems that we face in our everyday lives, and how the government has done nothing to alleviate these problems. They also talked about how the government is only furthering the class divisions within the society, and that there's a need for revolution. They explained to us about capitalistic society, and the government's involvement in promoting capitalism. Whatever they said made complete sense at least to me. If you listen to them, you will certainly agree with the ideals that they follow. Once the meeting was over, the party members had arranged for some cultural programmes. Whenever there's a meeting, you can expect some singing and dancing.'

About 75 kilometres away from Gumla is the Torpa block of Khunti district where the colour red has changed slightly in recent times.

These villages are controlled not by the banned CPI (Maoist) but the Peoples' Liberation Front of India (PLFI). The area came into the limelight because of the resistance against Koel-Karo dam project. Ronald was himself involved in the conflict.

'Something important that you must understand is that the people here, especially our tribal people, are hardly concerned about the future. They would rather spend their money today than save it for a better tomorrow. This is one of the main reasons why our people are not as well off as non-tribals. Most of us are little concerned about our children's future, so we don't save up. The thinking is that the new generation must build their own lives. Everyone starts their life from scratch. They inherit only poverty.'

'It is an unequal society in these parts but things are better in terms of communities living together. There are incidents of people from other communities trying to exert their power/influence on us, but there is resistance. If the party members are told of any such incidents of discriminatory practices, they take severe action. However, the tribal people themselves, without the party's help, are united and capable enough to fight against any such practices in some cases.'

'Our first successful struggle was against the setting up of the Koel-Karo project, which would have submerged more than 250 villages. It was in 1995. Since then, we have carried out several campaigns against any government efforts to restart this project. Every year on 5 July we commemorate these "struggles" and present a signed petition to the government to quash any plans of restarting this project for good.'

'In 1995, P.V. Narasimha Rao who was then the prime minister had publicly declared that he would be building the Koel-Karo dam at any cost. The project was supposed to be inaugurated in either the Torpa block or the place where the dam was to be built. At that time, Jharkhand and Bihar were one, and the then chief minister Lalu Yadav had claimed that if the prime minister does not inaugurate the project, he himself would do it. In protest, thousands, almost 45,000–50,000 gathered together, and subsequently set up a gatepost. No one, including the government officials and dam project employees, were allowed to that post without the villagers' consent. The protests made the government relent to their demands, and it suspended the project for the time being. Since then and up to this day, the villagers have consistently struggled against the restarting of the project.'

'But things took an ugly and violent turn in 2002. By then, the party members had established themselves in this area, especially on the Derang side (in the Khunti district of Jharkhand). A police team had gone for patrolling towards the Derang area; however, on their way back they broke the gate and carried it along with them to the police station. Two villagers went to the police station, asking them why they broke the gate, which was meant for villagers' safety against the project. The policemen, instead of listening, started beating these two men with rifle butts. As soon as the news spread, a huge mob gathered at the police station and started protesting. The incident took place on 1 February 2002, and the tribals surrounded the post on 2 February. The station in-charges of Raniya and Tapkara were both present at the scene. Soon the situation got tense; the police refused to relent. The village leaders then contacted the SP but before the SP could arrive, the policemen started firing. This incident happened under the orders of Babulal Marandi who was the first chief minister of Jharkhand. He had tried to do away with the Chotanagpur Tenancy Act (CNT Act) as well. However, the persistent "struggle" has ensured that the government could not modify or remove this Act.'[22]

'They tried to convince the villagers about building a smaller dam that would have less impact. But the government was told in as many words that they would not get even a single inch of this land. At the time of this incident, hundreds of government and project officials swarmed this place. The villagers used every possible means, all non-violent, to stop the officials from coming into these areas. The women would lead these protests, and everyone would sit on the road blocking the way. The officials were warned that if they even lay a finger on our women, rape charges would be filed against them. The women were at the forefront in damaging their vehicles; no one was to come into these areas without written permission. If males were involved there was a possibility that things could have gotten out of control, so they encouraged the women to lead the struggle.'

'All the officers were forced to move out of this place. As of now, there's hardly anything left of the project; however, there are some people who still want to pursue this project. The villagers often meet in Tapkara to discuss the agenda of forcing the government to shut down this project forever.'

'This is very significant because tribal Adivasi people are generally seen as a group who can't articulate their problems, can't protect their own interests like land and here they were fighting tooth and nail to preserve it. And guess what, there wasn't any external influence on any of these decisions. The people were acutely aware of the fact that this project would take away water, land and jungle resources; without them, they wouldn't be able to sustain livelihoods.'

'Our forefathers laboured day and night to make this place a home for us, so why would we let the government take it away from us?'

'The government officials no longer interfere in any of our protest movements. The face-off with the officials made it clear that the villagers would neither relent nor accept any interference.'

'The government is more or less absent. None of their programmes function properly. The nearby road was constructed in 2008–09, under the MNREGA scheme, and people are yet to receive payments for that. They dug some wells and a check dam; however, they haven't provided any means to irrigate the fields from the water resources. And the residents are completely dependent on missionary schools to get their children educated.'

'Though the police is now better behaved, they still do act the bully sometimes. A few years back when Masi Charan Purty was the zonal commander here, the police had caught someone named Masi from the market. They thought that the person in their custody was Masi Charan, and they tortured him for hours. It was only later revealed that the guy, except for a common name, had no links with the zonal commander. In fact, he was the brother of a police officer, a DSP. Once the DSP called and pulled up these policemen for wrongfully detaining and torturing his brother, they released him.

'This block is under PLFI. For the villagers, it is the same no matter who is in charge. There is some amount of fear among the villagers, but the party members have never troubled us. They are only against those people who have committed crimes or are police informants. If you haven't done anything wrong, you have no reason to fear them. Nevertheless, there are some young people who after getting drunk might threaten someone, but those incidents should not be construed as the party threatening the villagers. A few youngsters from the village and the surrounding ones have joined the party. The present zonal commander, Jidan Gudiya, was my classmate from the 6th till the 10th standard. His reasons for joining the party are completely different from other party members. He was quite good in studies. He was running a cloth shop, which made decent profits. For increasing his capital investment, he had taken a loan from the bank, but was not able to repay that amount. It was then that he joined the party.'

'When it comes to helping people, the party does provide monetary help during marriages in areas beyond Derang village. Apparently, they haven't yet forced anyone from the village or any other neighbouring villages to join the group. There are certain things that they are very strict about. For example, they don't ever spare any police informants. Recently, some months back, they killed two Muslim brothers who allegedly passed information to the DSP and the SP.'

'Many of the politicians have links with the party members. In the recent election, the party members clearly supported Enos Ekka (Jharkhand Party) from this place. Enos has a hold over this area, and the villagers here have a genuine liking for him. The party members had campaigned for him in several of the interior areas. There are other legislative assembly members as well who are directly linked with the party.'

'But yes, we feel like we are trapped between the two groups – the police and the party. If you support the police, the party will come after you and if you support the party, the police will come after you.'

Shanti Munda, Animesh and I

Uttor Bongo – North Bengal – Siliguri, Naxalbari have all been part of the growing up years of many of us. I never lived there but the landscape was familiar to so many of us; it evoked 'revolution'. The ground there has nothing left of the 1960s except the row of red monuments with busts of left leaders and a plaque with names of the 'martyrs' of that uprising adjacent to a school where the students are oblivious of their historical neighbourhood. A space between the second and third monuments is now used as a flag post, though all I saw was a bamboo pole without the red flag.

In one of the villages, I finally meet Shanti Munda who is at the riverbank and walks up to meet me. She was present the day of the great Naxalbari uprising when her comrades were killed in what they believed was a revolt. Today she says that sacrifice was meaningless.

But she still unwaveringly believes in 'land to the tiller'. She still tills her land. Standing straight, she looks me in the eye as she recalls how, on May 24 she led a group of women in Jhorjote to snatch land from a landlord. That was when policemen led by inspector Sonam Wangdi tried to stop them. That day Shanti was carrying her fifteen-day-old daughter on her back and saw Wangdi kicking a pregnant woman. She ordered her group to fire arrows and and didn't stop till she killed him. The pregnant woman died a few months later. Other accounts indicate Wangdi was killed with a single arrow. The next day, Shanti led the group to Bengai-jote when police opened fire, killing nine women, a man and a child. Naxalbari turned violent and Shanti became the commander with Kanu Sanyal calling the shots. Today she still believes in the extreme ideology but says murder of 'class enemies' without a trial was wrong.

That day's editorial in *The Statesman*, 27 May 1967, wasn't sure whether 'political extremists' played a role in the incident of killing of a police inspector. It suggested that 'Wednesday's attack on a police party was probably the result of a sudden outburst of inflammable tribal passions.' The next report appeared only on 31 May, which clearly said, 'The Phansidewa area of Siliguri sub-division comprising of Naxalbari, Khoribari and Phansidewa has been the scene of age old agrarian disputes in which forces of jotedars had been pitted against the land-hungry kisans and share croppers.'[23] By June, the government 'unanimously decided that there was no alternative but to let the army take over the affected areas, as reported in *The Statesman*, 3 June.[24]

Since 1959, the Krishak Sabha, the peasant union that mobilized peasants for land redistribution, has been active in these areas covering around 77 square kilometres and a population of 80,000. The active membership was reportedly around 6,000, of which more than 800 had warrants against them.

After Naxalbari, hundreds of youth like Samaresh Majumdar's fictional protagonist Animesh travelled to Calcutta and was sucked into the Naxalite movement that had spilled into the streets. It wasn't long before it would go awry following cracks in leadership and a brutal reign of crackdown by the government. Torture, custodial killings and staged encounters became routine and Animesh too ended up in jail, severely tortured and crippled from hip down.

The splintered Maoist groups have made repeated attempts to come together in the decades that have passed. The government has neither a policy nor any understanding of the movement. When the Maoists were not a force in the early 1990s in Odisha and the state was just a sanctuary for them, the Odisha government felt it was Andhra's problem. In ten years, the situation changed and the party gained considerable ground in Odisha. The dispossession of people from natural resources was bound to have an impact. But similar battles were taking place where the Maoists didn't exist. Thus, to conflate Adivasis with Maoists would be a gross mistake.

One of the things I have been trying to understand through this book is this dynamics. Are Adivasis with the Maoists? Yes, of course. While the majority of the Maoist cadres are drawn from the Adivasi tribes, I don't know of Adivasis ideologically theorizing a war against the state. The Maoists have a theorized war against the state. When Adivasis are fighting, they are doing so to defend resources, to defend his or her forest or even their way of life. They have been fighting for hundreds of years against various forms of exploitation but that is only to protect what is theirs and not against the state to usurp power. The Adivasi Maoist cadres I met in the course of researching for this book too had little idea of what was going on in the rest of the country or the world.

The Maoists, on the other hand, are clear about what they want in terms of theory. However, this comes with huge contradictions and dishonesty. For example, after the kidnapping of the collector in Malkangiri in 2011, the moment the Maoists got their cadres released and the alleged ransom from the government, they dropped all the other demands and left. At that point, they didn't care about all the issues they had raised regarding the villagers; basically, both the government and the Maoists deserted the people. This has been the story of the Maoist movement over the years and across all the districts they claim to have some presence. The Maoists enforce codes on people or the government hunts the same people down on one pretext or the other; neither ensures the interests of the civilians caught in a deadly battle of turf war over resource and power.

Whether through force or indifference, the nature of state response is bound up with the whole politics of dispossession, of throwing people out of their own land. Why the word 'resource' is important is because it is at the heart of the Maoist movement as well as of Adivasi resistance. The first response of the Indian state to any battle over resource has been to use force and criminalize the people demanding what has been granted to them by the Constitution.

In an email sent to me, historian and social scientist Ramachandra Guha pointed out that after Independence:

> Dalits, women and Muslims continued to be discriminated against. Yet, their problems were taken up by influential parties and politicians ... On the other hand, Adivasis, always neglected, became victims of a development process that rested on the exploitation of their lands, their forests, and their waters. In the 1950s and 1960s, they were displaced by mines, dams and logging projects conducted by the state; from the 1990s, by such projects executed by the private

sector. And still, no major political party took up the growing dispossession of Adivasis. It was in this vacant space that the Naxalites moved in.

The first response to any displacement battle is to criminalize the protestors. There are cases where children have been booked for attempt to murder. This kind of response not only dispossesses the family from their resources but sets them against the state that is meant to protect them. That is when the Maoists enter and pretend to protect the people and either indoctrinate them or just exploit their helplessness. And the state finds itself justified in using further force and brutalizing the entire population. The two issues – of Left Wing Extremism and Adivasi rights and resistance – are different and it is a huge error to mix them up because that in itself fuels the movement that has otherwise virtually lost moral and physical ground in terms of representing who they claim to be fighting for. Ramachandra Guha writes in his email, 'The Naxalites are often brutal in their methods. As a constitutional democrat, I detest them. At the same time, the roots of Naxalism lie in part in the tragic predicament of the Adivasis. Unless this question is squarely and systematically addressed, the violence will continue.'

Shanti Munda carries on working with the CPI (ML) with little or no hope for the rights for workers while Animesh has long reconciled with the death of the movement. Many 'comrades' have joined the establishment; many more were killed in staged encounters or have 'disappeared'. Though the movement manages to survive and sustain itself, the revolution remains unfinished.

Postscript

THOUGHTS ON THE ADIVASIS AND MAOISTS

Satyabrata Pal

Shortly after I joined the National Human Rights Commission (NHRC) in March 2009, I was given a list of districts, one in each state, which the organization had identified as of particular concern and monitored through inspection visits. I asked how these were chosen and was told that they had the poorest indicators for health, education, nutrition, sanitation, and therefore the human rights deficit was particularly high there.

Reports on these districts showed that almost all had high concentrations of Adivasis, and sometimes of Dalits as well. Quite a few had something else in common. There was a remarkable overlap between these districts, with their severe human rights deficit, and those identified by the Home Ministry as most completely under Maoist sway. It was hard not to come to the conclusion that the one had led to the other, that the Maoists were the product and the beneficiaries of years of neglect of areas and segments of India's population that needed the greatest nurturing and attention.

In Jamui in Bihar, there were several areas I could not go to, because the Maoists were active there. These included those where the Adivasis were concentrated, where the SP explained that he could not let me travel unescorted because the risk of a Maoist ambush was too high; if he sent a police escort, however, the Maoists would certainly attack. If these were no-go areas for government agencies, then anganwadis, schools, health centres weren't working or were being left to their own devices. Life in these Adivasi villages, already parlous, was getting even more precarious.

I found the same situation in Chhatra in Jharkhand. There, however, the SP took me to a remote village where the Maoists had recently demolished the school. He did so after establishing that the Maoists had now withdrawn further into the jungle, but even so, a road-opening party flanked the road as our convoy drove through. The villagers said the CRPF had stayed in the school during the last elections, though they had begged them not to; as soon as they left, the Maoists arrived and blew it up. But the Maoists are your people, I said; why did you let them? The village headman said, we don't have the guns; the Maoists and the police do; the men with the guns don't listen to us. This is a plaint I heard over and over again throughout the Maoist belt.

In the districts of the Bastar region in Chhattisgarh, the district magistrates confessed that the only centrally assisted programme that ran there was the PDS, which the Maoists allowed because it served several purposes for them: without the food, the Adivasis would die, depriving them of cadres and of local support, and a part of the supplies fed their *dalams* as well. It meant though that, here as elsewhere through much of the Maoist belt, the writ of the government did not run. Where it was trying, very tardily, to make amends for decades of neglect, the Maoists would not let it, or allow only what suited them.

Every visit to Adivasi habitations showed how acute that neglect had been. When Operation Anaconda was launched against the Maoists in central India, the NHRC received complaints that in a cluster of villages in Jharkhand government services had been shut down, putting the Adivasis to enormous suffering. The NHRC team sent to investigate had to trek through the Saranda forest, spending two nights in the open, to reach the villages: almost seventy years after independence, no roads led there. (In Bastar, the huge tract of forested hills where the Maoists operate is known as Abujhmar, literally terra incognita. Civil servants do not tread there; civic services are unknown.)

When the NHRC team reached the villagers, they heard that Anaconda had of course created its own difficulties, but the schools, primary health centres and anganwadis had hardly ever run, at the best of times. The government's crackdown had simply exacerbated a chronic problem of a denial of services: that was a creation of the state, not of the paramilitary or the Maoists, the protagonists in Anaconda.

An Expert Group set up by the Planning Commission to look at 'Development Challenges in Extremist Affected Areas' minced no words in its 2008 report. Though it ignored some of the tensions within the Maoist movement, it also stated bluntly that:

> In general, the contradiction between the tribal community and the State itself has become sharper, translating itself into open conflict in many areas. Almost all over the tribal areas, including Nagaland, Manipur, Tripura, Assam, Jharkhand, Orissa, Chhattisgarh, Maharashtra, Andhra Pradesh and

Kerala, tribal people seem to feel a deep sense of exclusion and alienation.

It went on to say:

> There is, however, a failure of governance, which has multiple dimensions and is not confined to the inefficiency of the delivery system only. It is not fortuitous that overwhelmingly large sections of bureaucracy/technocracy constituting the delivery system come from landowning dominant castes or well-to-do middle classes, with their attachment to ownership of property, cultural superiority, purity-pollution governed behaviour and a state of mind which rationalizes and asserts their existing position of dominance in relation to others.

And though it slurred over the different and sometimes contradictory needs of the Maoist support base, it asked that they:

> be recognised as a political movement with a strong base among the landless and poor peasantry and adivasis. Its emergence and growth need to be contextualised in the social conditions and experience of people who form a part of it. The huge gap between state policy and performance is a feature of these conditions ... Its geographical spread is rooted in failure to remove the conditions which give rise to it.

This report rots unread, neglected like the areas and the people to whose desperate plight it drew attention. Almost nothing has been done to 'remove the conditions which give rise' to the anger and alienation that bred the Maoists. States have looked at easier solutions. A ruthless paramilitary operation has defeated the Maoists in Andhra Pradesh, lulling it into a sense of arrogant complacency, though since the movement has been reincarnated more than once there, it should know that only a battle has been won, no more. The war has not, and hearts most certainly have not.

In Chhattisgarh, the state has been far more innovative, creating clusters in district headquarters where boarding schools have been set up for Adivasi children, who are plucked from the clutches of the Maoists, and study there from infancy until they graduate from school, after which they can, depending on aptitude, go on to colleges or to vocational training centres, set up in the same locations. None of the hundreds of Adivasi children I met wanted to return to their villages. All of them wanted to stay on where they were, but they had been cut off from, were forgetting and turning away from, their roots, their families and their traditions. Chhattisgarh's cunning plan is to solve the Maoist problem by ending the tribal way of life. That is even more draconian than the military solution that Andhra Pradesh sought.

It is also insidious, because the largest reserves of the ores that corporate India wants to mine are in the forests and hills where the Adivasis live and which they worship as gods. For Adivasis like the Dongria Kondhs in the Niyamgiri hills of Odisha, which hold bauxite that Vedanta wants to extract, destroying their god is both sacrilegious and suicidal. As long as they retain their tribal identity and beliefs, they will not agree to their deities being desecrated or sacrificed, any more than a devout Hindu will let his cows be killed in front of him. But if Adivasi children are deracinated, the next generation will lose their attachment to place and slough off their old religions, making it much easier for their habitats to be claimed for development. A culture developed over millennia is being eradicated along with the environment in which it was born and grew. India needs to develop, but this is a terrible price to exact. It is an exaction, moreover, from which the Maoists will not protect the Adivasis.

If, as the Expert Group noted, the Maoists had 'a strong base among the landless and poor peasantry and adivasis', that might seem odd, but it is not, because there are tensions between the leaders and the locals, and between the groups from which the cadres are drawn. Firstly, though the Maoists tapped into the anger and despair in the Adivasi belt to revive their movement, their leaders are almost all urban, and not from the tribes, college-educated, self-consciously irreligious upper-caste men from Andhra Pradesh and West Bengal, who exploit Adivasi alienation but do not understand tribal mores or empathize with them. For these men, the animism of the tribes might be quaint, but will be indulged only if it does not thwart their first objective, to strengthen their movement, which they can by extorting bribes from mining companies. Reports sent to the NHRC showed that these companies rarely had problems working in forests dominated by the Maoists, even where the Adivasis did not want them.

The Maoist leadership gets both money and explosives from the mines, as they do from the companies that build roads in the areas they control, the only other development work that they permit the states to carry out there, for motives that are diabolical and with outcomes almost Kafkaesque. Initially the Maoists violently opposed any attempt to build roads in areas where their absence, as in Saranda, Abuhjmar and throughout the tribal belt, made access hard and therefore gave them safe refuge. It was obvious, to them as to others, that though the states claimed they were reaching out at last to remote Adivasi settlements, these roads were being built to make it easier to launch operations against their sanctuaries. They then realized that letting some roads through served many purposes: they could tell the Adivasis that they were not stopping something meant for them, but they would decide which roads would be built and which companies would build them, showing the tribes and the state that nothing could be done without their consent. Only those roads would be built that would not threaten their strongholds, and they would get money and explosives from the builders.

Even more, once the roads were built and used by the police, convoys that forgot precautions would become easy targets, which would be blown up by cadres trained with the money extracted from the contractors and with the explosives they had been forced to supply. The state therefore was the source of both the money and the explosives used to kill its forces. And in a last Machiavellian twist, these ambushes would always be near an Adivasi settlement on which, with savage predictability, the survivors and reinforcements would wreak vengeance, driving the tribes even more from the state and into the arms of the Maoists. For the Maoist leadership, this cunning and cynical tactic makes complete sense, but the Adivasis, as always, are the victims.

The second fault line in the 'red corridor' runs between the Adivasis and the Dalits. As the Expert Group noted, both are put upon by the upper castes and are the natural constituency for the Maoists, which draws its rank and file from them, but there is a hierarchy of pain between them and their interests often diverge. As in the United States, where both the blacks and the Hispanics form the sub-class but the Hispanics are at the bottom of the pile, the Adivasis, particularly the forest-dwelling tribes of the Maoist belt, suffer even more than the Dalits, their needs are not the same, and when they are organized they are tutored to eye each other warily, as rivals vying for the attention and aid they both desperately need. Before the Maoists came the evangelists, Christian and Hindu, and their converts, in Kandhamal and elsewhere, are often at each other's throats. For the Adivasis the forest is their world, their god and their life, for the Dalits it is wood they would like to clear and sell, to turn the land to farming.

The Maoist leaders have no time for faith or the rifts it causes. Their interests are served, of course, by getting the oppressed to bury their differences and make common cause with them, but ideologically and as city folk they are closer to the concerns of the Dalits than those of the Adivasis, which may seem impossibly arcane and primitive. It is perhaps telling that one of the largest common platforms they forged is the Chasi Mulia Adivasi Sangh: the peasants and bonded labour come first, the Adivasis bring up the rear.

Though they are in the vanguard and beyond it when the Maoists take on the security forces. When I first heard the claim that the Maoists use Adivasis as human shields, I dismissed it as propaganda, but it came up throughout the red corridor, from officers at all levels, giving informal, frank accounts of their operations. All of them said that the human screens that approached them were not members of the *dalams* but unarmed men and women, who knew they were going to their deaths if the police opened fire. There is clearly some truth in this, but why would the Maoists do something so cruel, which would turn the Adivasis against them?

Perhaps because these were Adivasis who were never with them. The Adivasis are also a house divided, and the Maoists have preyed on and profited from these divisions. In Chhattisgarh, the hundreds of Adivasi families who still live in camps in Dantewada, protected by the police, owned land in their old villages. The Maoists turned other Adivasis who had less land or none – sometimes, they said, from their own families – against them, threw them out of their houses and off their lands, and killed those who resisted. These were the Adivasis whom the late Mahendra Karma, then with the CPI and, like many communist leaders, from a family of landlords, organized into the Jan Jagran Andolan which then morphed into the brutal Salwa Judum, until it was banned in 2011 by the Supreme Court, after which its members were simply designated as an Auxiliary Armed Police Force. In May 2015, in frightening déjà vu, Karma's son has announced a successor to Salwa Judum, which he has named the Vikas Sangharsh Samiti and across the border in Odisha, in April, the Malkangiri Adivasi Sangh has threatened armed opposition if the Maoists do not stop exploiting Adivasis.

The state and the Maoists fight over the Adivasis, in every sense. Theirs are the hearts and minds that must be won, but they are also trampled underfoot as this fight rages around them. Ages back, in another land and among other tribes, two women came to their king, claiming the same baby. The king ordered that the baby be cut in half to be shared between the two, and knew who the mother was because she would rather part with her child than have it slaughtered. The Adivasis of India, our Adivasis, are orphaned and they are being torn apart. They have no Solomon.

Annexure

Indira Gandhi on Tribal Rights, 1974

19-6-74

1. There is a growing unrest among tribals in various parts of the country. Numerous memoranda are being submitted by Member of Parliament and others in this regard. The problems mentioned in these memoranda, etc, are generally looked into by the Ministries/Departments as individual or isolated incidents. However the emphasis that we wish to give to the development of the tribal areas makes it necessary to take a more comprehensive look at the problem.

2. It is well known that the present unrest among tribals in mainly due to:

i) Land alienation
ii) Exploitation by 'outsiders', and
iii) Lack of development in tribal areas.

But if one goes to the root of these problems, interesting facts come to light. Moreover, they are not separate problems in themselves – and in order to tackle them successfully an integrated strategy is called for.

3. The problem of tribal communities can broadly be divided into three groups:

i) tribal areas in North-East excluding Manipur, Tripura and Plain Tribals in Assam;
ii) tribal belt in Central India, Manipur, Tripura and Assam; and
iii) dispersed tribal population

The North-East tribal situation differs from that in the rest of the country by virtue of i) comparative isolation; ii) continued protection of traditional rights in forest and land; iii) educational advancement; and iv) comparatively larger plan effort. The problem of exploitation and deprivation, which is plaguing the other areas, is largely absent. Here the main problem is in regard to developmental efforts. These small states tend to formulate programmes on the model of the bigger states with the result that the average tribal has not benefited much notwithstanding large investments.

4. In the rest of the country, tribal areas are parts of large States and there has been considerable intermingling. The new contact in the absence of adequate protective measures and ineffective enforcement of such measures, leads to exploitation, viz., indebtedness, bondage, land alienation and loss of control over other productive assets. Large areas still continue to be predominantly tribal. The more inaccessible areas are underdeveloped but are comparatively free from exploitation.

5. In areas where tribals have been reduced to a minority through immigration and dispersal, they have also been deprived of their control over productive assets. Thus, there is a qualitative difference between areas of tribal concentration and dispersed tribal population.

6. The problems of areas of tribal concentration are easier to solve since area-based planning with focus on development of tribal communities can be envisaged. The situation can be saved from further deterioration and tribals can be helped to develop according to their genius.

7. A scrutiny of the various letters and memoranda written by tribal MPs and others has provided interesting and useful material in understanding their problems. The problem of dispersed tribal population, as stated, is different but the other two groups have the problems of i) inadequacy of development effort, ii) increasing exploitation in various forms, and iii) indifferent administration. And now, when the Fifth Plan is being formulated it should not be difficult to give this problem the attention it deserves.

8. In respect of the development effort, the primary question that is usually raised is in regard to financial resources. In the Fifth Plan this problem is sought to be tackled by the device of the Sub Plan for areas of tribal concentration. So far the State Plan efforts have been much too small and the additive Central Assistance generally has been the only investment. The States have now been asked to give necessary weightage for these areas in their Plans. The Central Ministries have also been asked to prepare Sub Plans for these areas with some

weightage in their favour. An outlay of Rs. 200 crores (out of Rs. 500 crores for hill and tribal areas) is likely to be set apart for these areas. As many of the general programmes are not suitable for tribal areas, the sectoral authorities have been asked to adapt their programmes and, where necessary, take up new programmes in these areas. It is also proposed that the outlays for the tribal areas should be made non divertable. What is to be ensured now is that there is no resistance in the Ministries and States in adopting this approach. Once this is done, the financial resources will be adequate although the difference between the levels of investment in the North-East and other tribal areas will continue. However, disparity of investment may not be the real issue, as the size of investments will be unprecedented. The main task will be to ensure their proper utilization; otherwise investment of this order itself will result in dislocating the tribal economy.

9. In areas outside the North Eastern region, apart from proper utilisation of development funds highest priority has to be given to elimination of exploitation. Such of the policies of the State governments as are leading to exploitation or having an adverse effect on tribal economy have to be reviewed. It would be seen from the letters written by MPs and others from time to time that the following need special attention:

a) Excise: It is now generally accepted that the excise policy followed by the State Governments has resulted in exploitation. A Sub Committee of the Central Advisory Board on Prohibition, comprising Excise Ministers of States, which went into this question, has confirmed this finding. Some time ago a group of Members of Parliament had represented against sale of distilled liquor in tribal areas. They went to the extent of suggesting that the development outlays could be reduced if revenue considerations come in the way. The Central Advisory Board on Prohibition has endorsed the suggestion. At the meeting of the Board, the Excise ministers did raise the question of revenue but in view of the continuing exploitation it was agreed that compensation could not be a precondition for the change. The Scheduled Areas and Tribes Commission had made similar recommendations in 1961 but it is a pity that even though accepted by the Government these have remained unimplemented so far. Since the matter has been gone into in detail, an early decision on the new excise policy should be taken without any further delay.

b) The forest policy, which is intimately connected with the tribal economy, is progressively veering towards commercial exploitation unrelated to the local economy. In more backward areas it is giving rise to considerable tensions. This needs an urgent review.

c) The Licensing policy and project formulation for big industrial and mining complexes hardly take into account the local simple tribal situation. New vested interests are being created in these areas. A balanced relationship between traditional economy and the modernized sector has to be built by introducing an element of local participation wherever possible and advanced planning for all round development in the entire region.

d) Exploitation by traders and money lenders continues to be a serious problem. A unified credit-cum-marketing structure has been accepted in principle which may attend to all the needs including credit for production, consumption and social needs, supply of essential consumer commodities and purchase of agricultural and minor forest produce. However, for the tribal areas the State Governments, the Reserve Bank of India, cooperatives and other organisations concerned with this problem have to change their rigid stands on procedure and organizational structure.

10. Despite legal safeguards, land alienation continues to be a serious problem in tribal areas. Although enforcement of relevant laws is ineffective, the main reason for land alienation is the general economic condition of tribals for which the factors mentioned above are responsible to a great extent. Therefore, while the enforcement of land laws will have to be strengthened, that alone will not help in solving the problem. The importance of the above mentioned factors has to be viewed in this context.

11. The most critical input for tribal development is the quality of administration. The socio economic conditions of the tribals vary considerably from one area to another and from one community to the other. Administrative conventions, evolved over long periods in the past with reference to the local situations have been superseded by uniform procedures creating adverse effects on tribal population. The super imposition of general administrative structure, evolved for advanced areas, on the simple tribal areas has resulted in considerable confusion. There is over specialization, avoidable duplication, lack of coordination and diffusion of responsibility. As protective and developmental functions can be hardly distinguished in most of these areas, bifurcating of development and regulatory functions is premature. The simple tribal situation needs a simple administrative structure within the comprehension of the people.

12. But what is worse, by and large postings in tribal areas are regarded as "punishment" postings with the result that quality of personnel in these areas is generally indifferent. There is considerable exploitation by petty officials with the resultant lack of confidence in the local administration. To state the obvious, key functionaries must have sympathy for the tribal. The selection of the right type of personnel is necessary to improve the quality of administration. It is relevant to note that proviso to article 275(1) specifically provided for bringing up the level of administration of tribal areas. But not enough attention has been paid to this aspect.

13. The tribal development, which is carried on through the State Governments, is one of those fields in which the Constitution vests the Union Government with extensive power. The Constitution has a provision for making regulations in case of any legal difficulty and a provision for issuing direction to States to avoid any Centre State controversy. It makes expenditure for tribal development a charge and financial sanction for developmental schemes automatic under proviso to Article 275(1). But the Centre has not exercised this authority enough. In actual practice its role has been confined to making grants to the States for this purpose. Now that the Centre intends to provide a much higher outlay than in the past it is necessary in order to ensure proper utilization of these funds, that it takes a more positive role in the subject as a whole on the basis of a clear cut strategy.

Sd/-
(Indira Gandhi)

Notes

Author's Note

1. Samaresh Majumdar, *Kalbela* (Kolkata: Ananda Publishers, 1983). This was first serialized in the Bengali weekly *Desh*)

2. See Daniel J. Rycroft, *Representing Rebellion: Visual Aspects of Counter-insurgency in Colonial India* (New Delhi: Oxford University Press, 2006).

Part I

1. On 2 January 2006, the village near the Kalinganagar steel hub in Jajpur district of Odisha, witnessed police firing as tribals were protesting the construction of the boundary wall of the Tata steel plant project. Fourteen tribals were killed.

2. On 16 December 2000, three tribals were killed and 30 seriously injured after police fired on agitators protesting against bauxite mining and construction of alumina refinery by Utkal Alumina International Limited (UAIL) at Maikanch in Odisha's Rayagada district.

3. On 24 October 2001, as the tribals of Nagarnar in Chhattisgarh resisted land acquisition for setting up a steel plant, the police opened fire injuring 45 people, mostly women.

4. For administrative purposes, the British had divided the subcontinent into various agencies and presidencies, divisions and provinces.

Part II

1. Herman Kulke et al., *Imaging Odisha*, vol. 2 (Bhubaneswar: Odisha Prafulla Pathagar Publications, 2013) p. 276.

2. See W. W. Hunter, 'Jagannath', in *History of Orissa*, vol. 1 (London: Smith Elder, 1872) pp. 81–136, reprinted in N. K. Sahu, ed., *A History of Orissa*, vol. 1 (Calcutta: Sushil Gupta, 1956) pp. 3 – 39; S. K. Panda, 'Evolution of Jagannath Cult', in P. K. Mishra, ed., *Comprehensive History and Culture of Orissa*, vol. 1 (New Delhi: Kaveri Books, 1997) p. 542.

3. Verrier Elwin, *The Oxford India Elwin* (London: Oxford University Press, 2008).

Part III

1. It was a 13-point charter of demands. The conditions included a halt to anti-Naxal operations, withdrawal of cases against tribal people lodged in jails in the name of Maoists and implementation of the 'agreement' with the rebels for the release of the then collector of Malkangiri district, Vineel Krishna, in February 2011.

Part IV

1. Verrier Elwin, *The Tribal World of Verrier Elwin: An Autobiography* (London: Oxford University Press, 1964).

2. Ibid.

3. Ibid.

4. See Report of the High Level Committee on Socio-economic, Health and Educational Status of Tribal Communities of India, Ministry of Tribal Affairs, May 2014, http://www.

indiaenvironmentportal.org.in/files/file/Tribal%20Committee%20 Report,%20May-June%202014.pdf

5. See the website of the High Level Committee on Status of Tribal Communities, Ministry of Tribal Affairs, http://hlc.tribal.nic.in/content/4_1_ImportantReports.aspx

6. Popularly known as DMB, Donkada Bhuvana Mohana Patnaik was with the undivided CPI and later the CPI (M), before joining the revolutionary communists in the Srikakulam Girijan Naxalbary Movement during 1960s. He was convener of the coordination committee of the Orissa State communist revolutionaries formed in 1968 and joined the CPI (ML) which came into existence later. He was one of the accused in the Parvathipuram conspiracy case during which he argued the case himself.

7. Sumanta Banerjee, *In the Wake of Naxalbari: A History of the Naxalite Movement in India* (Calcutta: Subarnarekha, 1980).

8. In 2011, the Collector of Koraput, Vineel Krishna, was abducted by the CPI (Maoists).

9. See interview with Comrade Ganapathy, General Secretary of the CPI (Maoist) on Comrade Azad, Politburo member and party spokesperson, *Nobody Can Kill the Ideas of 'Azad'! Nobody Can Stop the Advancement of the Revolution!!*, November 2010.

10. J. C. Price, *The Chuar Rebellion*, Census 1951, West Bengal: District Handbook, Midnapur, Appendix iv, p. clvi.

11. Cited in *Bengal Hurkaru*, 11 January 1833 by J C Jha from *The Bhumij Revolt* (Delhi: Munshiram Manoharlal Publishers Pvt. Ltd., 1967), p. 95.

12. W. W. Hunter, *The Annals of Rural Bengal* (New York: Leypoldt and Holt, 1868).

13. Ibid., p. 230.

14. From the account of Major F. W. Burroughs who had led the expedition and lost.

15. Somnath Hore, *Tebhaga: An Artists Diary and Sketchbook* (Calcutta: Seagull, 1990)

16. J. J. Roy Burman, 'Adivasi: A Contentious Term to Denote Tribes as Indigenous Peoples of India', *Mainstream Weekly*, vol. XLVII, no. 32, 25 July 2009, https://www.mainstreamweekly.net/article1537.html

17. Dairy of R.I. Richardson, Collector, Birbhum, September 1855, *Santhal Rebellion: Collected Documents* (Kolkata: Basumati, 1996); District Handbooks: West Bengal, Vol. 2 of District Handbooks (Kolkata: S. N. Guha Ray, 1954).

18. Refers to the tenure of the members of the lineage (khunt) who reclaimed lands (katti). It is an ancient tribal land settlement pattern where when a village got overcrowded, the heads would decide on another uninhabited place.

19. Sumanta Banerjee, ed., *Thema Book of Naxalite Poetry* (Calcutta: Thema, 1987) p. 15.

20. The 1971 uprising in which 788 members of the CPI(ML) were killed outside the jails in West Bengal between March 1970 and August 1971, and 42 (unofficially 172) inside the jails in Midnapore, Berhampore, Alipore, Dum Dum and Howrah, see *Frontier*, vol. 5, no. 40, 13 January 1973, pp 3-4.

21. In 1855, the Santhal uprising against the British was one of the fiercest. It marked a turning point in colonial policies. Several hundreds were killed, many Santhal villages were burnt down in brutal counter military expeditions. Sidhu died in that conflict. His three brothers were captured, tried and hanged. Soon after, another messianic movement took birth called the Kherwar movement, taking its name from the original name of the Santhal known as Kherwar (villager). This movement mobilized the Santhals around the belief that the present situation was a result of abandoning the worship of god and spirits. This was led by Bhagrit, a Santhal who in 1871 became a religious teacher. He also reminded his tribesmen that the land belonged to them and nobody had the right to tax it. He would pass around a bowl of rice asking who created it, his followers would say god and then he would ask who had ploughed the ground

and sown the seed, and the Santhals would rise in chorus saying, 'we'. But even before he could lead a revolt, he was arrested and thrown into jail. 'Messianic Movements in Primitive India', Stephen Fuchs, *Asian Folklore Studies*, vol. 24, no. 1 (Nagoya: Nanzan University, 1965) pp. 11-62.

22. However, in 2017, the state government amended three sections and abolished one sub-section of the Chotanagpur Tenancy Act (CNT), while one section of Santhal Pargana Tenancy Act (SPT) has been amended.

23. 'Land Disputes Behind Naxalbari Incidents', *The Statesman*, 31 May 1967.

24. 'Army Takeover of Naxalbari Suggested', *The Stateman*, 3 June 1967.

References

Banerjee, Sumanta, ed., *Thema Book of Naxalite Poetry* (Calcutta: Thema, 2009).

Banerjee, Sumanta, *In the Wake of Naxalbari: A History of the Naxalite Movement in India* (Calcutta: Subarnarekha, 1980).

Duyker, Edward, *Tribal Guerrillas: Santhals of West Bengal and the Naxalite Movement* (New Delhi: Oxford University Press, 1987).

Elwin, Verrier, *The Tribal Art of Middle India: A Personal Record* (London: Oxford University Press, 1951)

Elwin, Verrier, *Leaves from the Jungle: Life in a Gond Village* (London: John Murray, 1936).

Elwin, Verrier, *The Tribal World of Verrier Elwin: An Autobiography* (London: Oxford University Press, 1964).

Ghosh, Suniti Kumar, ed., *The Historic Turning-Point: A Liberation Anthology*, vol. 2 (Calcutta: S. K. Ghosh, 1993).

Hunter, W. W., *The Annals of Rural Bengal* (New York: Leypoldt and Holt, 1868).

Hunter, W. W., 'Jagannath', in *History of Orissa*, vol. 1 (London: Smith Elder, 1872), reprinted in N. K. Sahu, ed., *A History of Orissa*, vol. 1 (Calcutta: Sushil Gupta, 1956).

Kulke, Hermann et al., *Imaging Odisha*, vol. 2 (Bhubaneswar: Odisha Prafulla Pathagar Publications, 2013).

Panda, S. K., 'Evolution of Jagannath Cult', in P. K. Mishra, ed., *Comprehensive History and Culture of Orissa*, vol. 1 (New Delhi: Kaveri Books, 1997).

Rycroft, Daniel J., *Representing Rebellion: Visual Aspects of Counter-insurgency in Colonial India* (New Delhi: Oxford University Press, 2006).

Singh, K. S., *Birsa Munda and His Movement 1874-1901: A Study of a Millenarian Movement in Chhotangpur* (New Delhi: Oxford University Press, 1983).

Watts, Neville A., *The Half-clad Tribals of Eastern India* (Bombay: Orient Longman, 1970).

Acknowledgements

Like most books of nonfiction this too has many authors. Though I had carried out my fieldwork in 2011 and 2014 while researching the Adivasi–Maoist relationship, this book is primarily the result of my excursions to Kandhamal in 2012 covering the abduction of the two Italian tourists. Claudio Colangelo, one of the hostages, shared the story of his abduction with me, painstakingly recounting the ordeal almost real time; that perspective has added a dimension we would have otherwise lacked. Elena Frova shared what was going on back home in Rome while Claudio was in the custody of the Maoists. Claudio has been in regular touch with me and has responded whenever I wanted to clarify anything related to the book. His experience of 2012 hasn't changed his love for India and every year he has been visiting the country, trying to help some of the people he encountered in the villages before his abduction. I did not meet Paolo either in custody or after his release and when I tried to contact him later he was withdrawn and refused to speak about the incident. The Maoist commander Sabyasachi Panda's long conversations with Claudio and me also contribute to understanding the contradictions within the CPI (Maoist) today. Panda is now in jail.

I must acknowledge my crew and colleagues who accompanied me in this journey, particularly Sampad Mahapatra without whom we couldn't have gone there. I owe to him much of my understanding on the issue. I must thank my cameraperson Biswajit Das who patiently documented the stories even though conditions were extremely harsh. A huge thanks to NDTV, where I spent more than seventeen exciting years and which allowed me to venture almost anywhere I wanted to.

Daringbari was central to the coverage not just of the abduction but of getting access to the Maoist corridor and that was made possible because of Kailash Dandapat's hospitality and guidance. He was with us at almost every step and when we returned from the jungles, it was he who made the broadcast possible, making logistical arrangements.

Every person I met in the course of this coverage, including the Maoist cadres, has contributed in the writing of this book and helping to understand the complex and troubled relationship between one of most impoverished yet richest regions of the country and half-century old armed movement that has been India's acknowledged 'biggest internal security threat'.

I am grateful to Richard Toppo, a research fellow I befriended during my stint at IDSA who helped me with the field research of the section 'Jal, Jameen, Jungle: 2014'.

The time of the reportage was also a time of personal tribulations and I must thank the people who stood by me then.

I may not have written this book if Rajdeep Mukherjee of Pan Macmillan India and Pranav Kumar Singh didn't ask me to. I thank my editors, Pooja Pandey, Sushmita Chatterjee, Rimli Barooah and publisher Diya Kar Hazra, who helped give the book shape.

I must thank Ramachandra Guha for his encouragement and for his note to me on the major issue the book grapples with: the Adivasi–Maoist relationship. My discussions and correspondence with P. Sainath on this very dynamics was extremely valuable. My gratitude is to Satyabrata Pal who agreed to write the postscript to the book, bringing in his personal and professional experiences and perspectives. His recent ill health has not allowed him to go through or update his essay that was written in 2015.